The Dart Programming Language

The Dart Programming Language

Gilad Bracha

♦♦Addison-Wesley

Boston • Columbus • Indianapolis • New York • San Francisco • Amsterdam • Cape Town
Dubai • London • Madrid • Milan • Munich • Paris • Montreal • Toronto • Delhi • Mexico City
Sao Paulo • Sidney • Hong Kong • Seoul • Singapore • Taipei • Tokyo

For information about buying this title in bulk quantities, or for special sales opportunities (which may include electronic versions; custom cover designs; and content particular to your business, training goals, marketing focus, or branding interests), please contact our corporate sales department at corpsales@pearsoned.com or (800) 382-3419.

For government sales inquiries, please contact governmentsales@pearsoned.com.

For questions about sales outside the United States, please contact international@pearsoned.com.

Visit us on the Web: informit.com/aw

Library of Congress Control Number: 2015953614

ISBN-13: 978-0-321-92770-5
ISBN-10: 0-321-92770-2
Text printed in the United States on recycled paper at RR Donnelley in Crawfordsville, Indiana.
First printing, December 2015

To my mother, Shoshana,
who taught me to be picky.

Contents

Foreword

In the early spring of 2006, I wrote a short blog post called "Gilad is Right" where, as a recovering typaholic, I admitted that Gilad's idea of optional and layered type systems, where static types cannot change the runtime behavior of the program and do not prevent an otherwise legal program from compiling or executing, was a necessary design trade-off for programming languages aimed at millions of developers. At that time I was working on Visual Basic, which already supported a form of optional typing by means of the **Option Strict Off** statement, but that feature was under heavy fire from static typing proponents. Type systems are often highly non-linear and after a certain point their complexity explodes while adding very little value to the developer and making life miserable for the language implementors. Optional and layered type systems enable a much more gradual approach by allowing strong static typing to coexist peacefully with dynamic typing. Now nearly a decade later, the vision Gilad pioneered has become mainstream under the name *gradual typing*. Many programming languages that have been created in the last few years, such as Hack, TypeScript, Flow, Racket, and of course Dart, are gradually typed. Even academics have embraced the idea and write papers about it with frivolous titles that include words such as "threesomes" and "blame."

Another pragmatic aspect of Dart, but one that language purists have not yet accepted, is the fact that the Dart type system is deliberately unsound. In normal English this means that the Dart type checker will not flag certain type errors at compile time, but relies on runtime checking instead to ensure type safety. The main source of type unsoundness in Dart is covariant generics. To explain what variance is, let's first look at a vending machine from which we can only take drinks. If a cafeteria requires a vending machine with soda pop, we can legally install a vending machine that dispenses root beer since root beer is a type of soda pop (but it is illegal to install a vending machine for soda pop where a vending machine for root beer is required). In programming language speak we say that vending machines are *covariant*. Next let's take a look at garbage cans into which we can throw only garbage. If a cafeteria requires a garbage can for recyclables, we can legally install a garbage can for trash since recyclable garbage is a type of trash (but it is illegal to install a garbage can for recyclables where a garbage can for trash is required). In programming language speak we say that garbage cans are *contravariant*. If you are a little puzzled about contravariance you are not the only one, and you will appreciate Dart's decision to make all generic types covariant. The consequence of that choice is that if you need a garbage can for trash, you can legally install a garbage can for recyclables, but that garbage can will reject all non-recyclable trash that people are trying to dump in it. While theoretically unsound, unsafe variance actually feels rather natural for most developers, and I applaud the choice the Dart designers made here. As anyone that has struggled with ? **super** and ? **extends** can attest, languages that have chosen in favor of static type safety for generics do so at the expense of their users.

The Dart language designers made additional pragmatic choices that make coding in Dart a smooth experience. For example Dart has no interfaces, abstract base classes, or "normal" classes. Instead Dart only has classes that can be used as interfaces by implementing them, or used as base classes by extending them, or have their implementation reused by mixing them in. Every type in Dart is an object, so there is no difference between primitive (e.g., numeric) types and regular object types. Even though everything in Dart is an object, it is possible to define top-level functions and variables, so one no longer needs the dreaded **public static void** main incantation inside a top-level class to get going. Dart allows user-defined arithmetic operators, but does not support type-based overloading of methods. This significantly simplifies the language. In other programming languages that do support type-based overloading, the exact semantics of that feature often take up an unjustifiably large fraction of the language specification. Null-aware operators (even **null** is a normal object) and cascades give more power to the dot and make every API fluent for the user with little effort from the API writer.

While Dart is essentially a dynamic language because all types are optional, you will encounter far fewer "wat" moments than with most other dynamic languages. There is **null** but no **undefined**, and hence only == but no ===. Only **true** is true, so no more (foo && foo.bar()) to check for **null**. Dart has regular integer and floating point numeric types, without the mind-blowing runtime type conversions around + and == that make great exam questions, entertaining conference presentations, but frustrating bugs.

In my opinion, though obviously I am biased, what puts Dart right at the top of my favorite programming languages is that it is the only language that I know of that supports all four essential effects of programming:

	One	Many
sync	$\{ \dots$ **return** $e; \dots \}$	**sync*** $\{ \dots$ **yield** $e; \dots$ **for()** $\dots \}$
async	**async** $\{ \dots$ **await** $e \dots \}$	**async*** $\{ \dots$ **await** $e \dots$ **yield** $e; \dots \}$ **async*** $\{ \dots$ **await for()** $\dots \}$

That is, Dart has deep support for producing and consuming synchronous data streams (Iterable<T>) using generators and for loops inside **sync*** blocks, producing and consuming futures (Future<T>) using **await** expressions inside **async** blocks, and last but not least support for producing and consuming asynchronous data streams (Stream<T>) using asynchronous generators and for loops inside **async*** blocks. Built-in support for asynchronous programming is essential in any modern programming language, where even data in memory, let alone data across the network, is "far away" and imposes such high latency that synchronous access is prohibitively expensive. Like JavaScript, but unlike other languages that support generators, Dart has so-called delegating generators that avoid quadratic blowup of nested and recursively generated streams.

Despite all these nice touches, Dart is essentially a rather boring language by design. Thanks to support for getters, setters, lambdas, enums, reified generics, modules, an extensive well-crafted standard library, and a snappy package manager, Dart will feel comfortable, like well-worn shoes, if you are a developer coming from Java or C#, and feel like a breath of fresh air when coming from Javascript. This book will help you to understand the why, how, and what of all of Dart's features in Gilad's signature painstaking detail and inimitable style and get you productive in Dart in no time.

Erik Meijer
Palo Alto, California
October 2015

Preface

How is this book different from other books on Dart? Other books on Dart are full of practicalities; this book is focused on principles and ideas.

The practicalities of Dart are very important, but they are different this year than they were last year, and will likely differ again the year afterwards. In contrast, the principles behind Dart should be more applicable over time. You should read this book if you are interested in the ideas that motivate the design of the language, and how they manifest in the pragmatic, demanding real-world setting that is Dart.

One of the chief ideas in Dart is optional typing. I started working on optional types decades ago; today we see a proliferation of optional type systems, which I find immensely satisfying. While neither Dart nor any of its competitors realize optional types exactly as I would like them to, the fact that the idea has hit the mainstream is what matters.

Even more important is the idea that Dart is an object-oriented language, not in the conventional sense of classes, inheritance and the other standard paraphernalia known to most programmers, but in the deep sense that only the observable behavior of an object matters. Again, this idea is realized imperfectly, but better than in most mainstream languages.

Another key idea covered in this book is reflection. The topic of reflection is not well addressed by books on programming. For that reason, I was very keen to discuss reflection in this book. However, the history of reflection in Dart has been unexpectedly tortuous.

On the one hand, many of Dart's users have been eager to use reflection, sometimes for purposes it is not ideal for. On the other hand, certain current platforms are severely limited as compilation targets for Dart, and make reflection support relatively expensive, especially with respect to program size. This tension put Dart reflection in an awkward spot.

The sensitivity to code size and reflection's effect on it were well understood from the beginning. The problem and its solutions were discussed in the very first design document for Dart reflection in November 2011. Nevertheless it took some four years until the solution was realized in a form that programmers could easily apply.

I hope this book conveys these ideas and others effectively, but that is for you, the reader, to judge. It is possible that one could do better using a more purist language, but on the other hand it's not clear one would reach as large an audience. Perhaps someday I will try that experiment and see.

This book has been a long time coming. I delayed finishing the book until I could tell a reasonably cohesive story about reflection. Another reason for the delay is that the book's topic has evolved so rapidly that it was constantly at risk of being out of date. That risk has not passed, but at some point one needs to say "enough is enough."

Dart is an imperfect realization of the ideas that drove its design. No one is more aware of this fact than its designers. Nevertheless, it is a real language, in which millions of lines of mission-critical code have been written. It has moved the culture of programming forward in some ways, most notably in the area of optional typing. As they say in Denmark: It could have been worse.

Acknowledgments

The Dart programming language is the result of a large team effort. My work on Dart has been made much more pleasant because it has involved many colleagues who have been a pleasure to work with, many of whom are not only co-workers but friends. It has been my privilege to document some of this effort in this book, as well as via the Dart Language Specification.

The Dart language was conceived and designed by Lars Bak and Kasper Lund, and so this book literally could not exist without them. Lars is a longtime friend and colleague who has led the Dart project from its beginning. Among other things, Lars got me involved with Dart, and for that I owe him special thanks. Both Lars and Kasper are not only phenomenally talented systems designers and implementors, but fun to be with as well!

Special thanks also to Erik Meijer; working with him on the asynchronous features of Dart was a joy. Erik is a real programming language professional, of a caliber one meets only rarely.

If Chapter 8 owes a lot to Erik, Chapter 7 owes much to Ryan Macnak, who implemented mirrors in the Dart VM, to Peter Ahé, who pioneered them in dart2js, and to Erik Ernst, who worked on the reflectable library.

My work on the book you hold in your hands was supported not only by Lars, but also by my manager Ivan Posva. For the past four years I have shared office space with Ivan and the other members of the VM team in Mountain View: Zachary Anderson, Daniel Andersson, Siva Annamalai, Régis Crelier, Matthias Hausner, Ryan Macnak, John McCutchan, Srdjan Mitrovic and Todd Turnidge. I thank them for the pleasant company.

My frequent visits to Dart supreme headquarters in Aarhus, Denmark, have always been fun (even if the actual travel was not). The administrative support of Linda Lykke Rasmussen has been priceless.

My work on the Dart specification is the direct basis for this book. That work has benefited from the careful critiques of many people, but none more than Lasse Nielsen whose phenomenal attention to detail has caught many subtle issues.

I've also been heavily involved in the process of standardizing Dart. Anders Sandholm has shielded me from much of the burdens involved therein; I owe him for that. I also thank the other participants in the Dart standards committee, ECMA TC52.

Dart would not be possible without the work of many other Dart team members past and present. They are too numerous to list but they have all contributed to making Dart what it is today.

My longtime editor, Greg Doench, has always been exceedingly patient and a pleasure to work with.

As always, my wife, Weihong, and my son, Teva, make it all worthwhile.

Gilad Bracha
Los Altos, California
November 2015

About the Author

Gilad Bracha is a software engineer at Google where he works on Dart. In prior lives he has been a VP at SAP Labs, a Distinguished Engineer at Cadence, and a Computational Theologist and Distinguished Engineer at Sun. He is the creator of the Newspeak programming language, co-author of the Java Language and Virtual Machine Specifications, and a researcher in the area of object-oriented programming languages. Prior to joining Sun, he worked on Strongtalk, the Animorphic Smalltalk System. He received his B.Sc. in Mathematics and Computer Science from Ben Gurion University in Israel and a Ph.D. in Computer Science from the University of Utah.

Chapter 1

Introduction

Dart is a general purpose programming language. It is a new language in the C tradition, designed to be familiar to the vast majority of programmers. The obligatory "Hello World" example illustrates how familiar Dart syntax is:

```
main(){
  print('Hello World');
}
```

Unless your background in programming and computer science is either extremely unusual, or lacking entirely, this code should be virtually self-explanatory. We will of course elaborate on this program and more interesting ones in the pages that follow.

Dart is purely object-oriented, class-based, optionally typed and supports mixin-based inheritance and actor-style concurrency. If these terms are unfamiliar, fear not, they will all be explained as we go along.

That said, this book is not intended as a tutorial for novices. The reader is expected to have a basic competence in computer programming.

While the bulk of this book will describe and illustrate the semantics of Dart, it also discusses the rationale for certain features. These discussions are included because, in my experience, good programmers are interested not only in what a programming language does, but why. And so, the next few sections give a very high level overview of the philosophy behind Dart. Later sections will also incorporate discussions of design decisions, alternatives and the history of the key ideas. However, if you are eager to just dive in, section 1.4 gives a quick tutorial.

And now, on with the show!

1.1 Motivation

The rise of the world-wide web has changed the landscape of software development. Web browsers are increasingly seen as a platform for a wide variety of software applications. In recent years, mobile devices such as smartphones and tablets have also become increasingly ubiquitous. Both of these trends have had a large impact on the way software is written.

Web browsers started as a tool to display static hypertext documents. Over time, they evolved to support dynamic content. Dynamic content is computed and recomputed over time and has grown from simple animations to server-based applications such as database front-ends and store fronts for internet commerce to full-fledged applications that can run offline.

This evolution has been organic; a series of accidents, some happy and some less so, have enabled such applications to run on an infrastructure that was not really designed for this purpose.

Mobile applications pose their own challenges. These applications must conserve battery life, providing a new incentive to improve performance. Network access may be slow, costly or even absent. Mobile platforms tend to impose a particular life cycle with particular restrictions on size.

Dart is intended to provide a platform that is specifically crafted to support the kinds of applications people want to write today. As such it strives to protect the programmer from the undesirable quirks and low-level details of the underlying platform while providing easy access to the powerful facilities new platforms have to offer.

1.2   Design Principles

1.2.1   Everything Is an Object

Dart is a pure object-oriented language. That means that all values a Dart program manipulates at run time are objects—even elementary data such as numbers and Booleans. There are no exceptions.

Insisting on uniform treatment of all data simplifies matters for all those involved with the language: designers, implementors and most importantly, users.

For example, collection classes can be used for all kinds of data, and no one has to be concerned with questions of autoboxing and unboxing. Such low-level details have nothing to do with the problems programmers are trying to solve in their applications; a key role of a programming language is to relieve developers of such cognitive load.

Perhaps surprisingly, adopting a uniform object model also eases the task of the system implementor.

1.2.2   Program to an Interface, not an Implementation

The idea that what matters about an object is how it behaves rather than how it is implemented is the central tenet of object-oriented programming. Unfortunately this tenet is often ignored or misunderstood.

Dart works hard to preserve this principle in several ways, though it does so imperfectly.

- Dart types are based on interfaces, not on classes. As a rule, any class can be used as an interface to be implemented by other classes, irrespective of whether the two share implementation (there are a few exceptions for core types like numbers, Booleans and strings).

- There are no final methods in Dart. Dart allows overriding of almost all methods (again, a very small number of built-in operators are exceptions).

- Dart abstracts from object representation by ensuring that all access to state is mediated by accessor methods.

- Dart's constructors allow for caching or for producing instances of subtypes, so using a constructor does not tie one to a specific implementation.

As we discuss each of these constructs we will expand on their implications.

1.2.3   Types in the Service of the Programmer

There is perhaps no topic in the field of programming languages that generates more intense debate and more fruitless controversy than static typechecking. Whether to use types in a programming language is an important design decision, and like most design decisions, involves trade-offs.

On the positive side, static type information provides valuable documentation to humans and computers. This information, used judiciously, makes code more readable, especially at the boundaries of libraries, and makes it easier for automated tools to support the developer.

Types simplify various analysis tasks, and in particular can help compilers improve program performance.

Adherents of static typing also argue that it helps detect programming errors.

Nothing comes for free, and adding mandatory static type checking to a programming language is no exception. There are, invariably, interesting programs that are prohibited by a given type discipline. Furthermore, the programmer's workflow is often severely constrained by the insistence that all intermediate development states conform to a rigid type system. Ironically, the more expressive the type discipline, the more difficult it is to use and understand. Often, satisfying a type checker is a burden for programmers. Advanced type systems are typically difficult to learn and work with.

Dart provides a productive balance between the advantages and disadvantages of types. Dart is an optionally typed language, defined to mean:

- Types are syntactically optional.

- Types have no effect on runtime semantics.

Making types optional accommodates those programmers who do not wish to deal with a type system at all. A programmer who so chooses can treat Dart as an ordinary dynamically typed language. However, all programmers benefit from the extra documentation provided by any type annotations in the code. The annotations also allow tools to do a better job supporting programmers.

Dart gives warnings, not errors, about possible type inconsistencies and oversights. The extent and nature of these warnings is calibrated to be useful without overwhelming the programmer.

At the same time, a Dart compiler will never reject a program due to missing or inconsistent type information. Consequently, using types never constrains the developer's workflow. Code that refers to declarations that are absent or incomplete may still be productively run for purposes of testing and experimentation.

The balance between static correctness and flexibility allows the types to serve the programmer without getting in the way.

The details of types in Dart are deferred until Chapter 5, where we explain the language's type rules and explore the trade-offs alluded to above in detail.

1.3 Constraints

Dart is a practical solution to a concrete problem. As such, Dart's design entails compromises. Dart has to run efficiently on top of web browsers as they exist today.

Dart also has to be immediately recognizable to working programmers. This has dictated the choice of a syntax in the style of the C family of programming languages. It has also dictated semantic choices that are not greatly at variance with the expectations of mainstream programmers. The goal has not been radical innovation, but rather gradual, conservative progress.

As we discuss features whose semantics have been influenced by the above constraints, we shall draw attention to the design trade-offs made. Examples include the treatment of strings, numbers, the return statement and many more.

1.4 Overview

This section presents a lightning tour of Dart. The goal is to familiarize you with all the core elements of Dart without getting bogged down in detail.

Programming language constructs are often defined in a mutually recursive fashion. It is difficult to present an orderly, sequential explanation of them, because the reader needs to know all of the pieces at once! To avoid this trap, one must first get an approximate idea of the language constructs, and then revisit them in depth. This section provides that approximation.

After reading this section, you should be able to grasp the essence of the many examples that appear in later sections of the book, without having read the entire book beforehand.

Here then, is a simple expression in Dart:

```
3
```

It evaluates, unsurprisingly, to the integer 3. And here are some slightly more involved expressions:

```
3 + 4
(3+4)*6
1 + 2 * 2
1234567890987654321 * 1234567890987654321
```

These evaluate to 7, 42, 5 and 15241578774577047232281664377899710041 respectively. The usual rules of precedence you learned in first grade apply. The last of these examples is perhaps of some interest. Integers in Dart behave like mathematical integers. They are not limited to some maximal value representable in 32 or 64 bits for example. The only limit on their size is the available memory.[1]

Dart supports not just integers but floating-point numbers, strings, Booleans and so on. Many of these built-in types have convenient syntax:

```
3.14159 //  A floating-point number
'a string'
"another string - both double quoted and single quoted forms are supported"
'Hello World' // You've seen that already
true
false //  All the Booleans you'll ever need
[] // an empty list
[0, 1.0, false, 'a', [2, 2.0, true, "b"]] // a list with 5 elements, the last of which is a list
```

As the above examples show, single-line comments are supported in Dart in the standard way; everything after // is ignored, up to the end of the line. The last two lines above show literal lists. The first list is empty; the second has length 5, and its last element is another literal list of length 4.

Lists can be indexed using the operator []

```
[1, 2, 3] [1]
```

The above evaluates to 2; the first element of a list is at index 0, the second at index 1 and so on. Lists have properties length and isEmpty (and many more we won't discuss right now).

```
[1, 2, 3]. length // 3
[].length // 0
[].isEmpty // true
['a'].isEmpty // false
```

One can of course define functions in Dart. We saw our first Dart function, the main() function of "Hello World", earlier. Here it is again

```
main(){
  print('Hello World');
}
```

Execution of a Dart program always begins with a call to a function called main(). A function consists of a header that gives its name and any parameters (our example has

---

1. Some Dart implementations may not always comply with this requirement. When Dart is translated to Javascript, Javascript numbers are sometimes used to represent integers since Javascript itself does not support an integer datatype. As a result, integers greater than 2^{53} may not be readily available.

none) followed by a body. The body of main() consists of a single statement, which is a call to another function, print() which takes a single argument. The argument in this case is the string literal 'Hello World'. The effect is to print the words "Hello World".

Here is another function:

```
twice(x) => x * 2;
```

Here we declare twice with a parameter x. The function returns x multiplied by 2. We can invoke twice by writing

```
twice(2)
```

which evaluates to 4 as expected. The function twice consists of a signature that gives its name and its formal parameter x, followed by => followed by the function body, which is a single expression. Another, more traditional way to write twice is

```
twice(x) {
    return x * 2;
}
```

The two samples are completely equivalent, but in the second example, the body may consist of zero or more statements—in this case, a single **return** statement that causes the function to compute the value of x*2 and return it to the caller.

As another example, consider

```
max(x, y){ if (x > y) return x; else return y; }
```

which returns the larger of its two arguments. We could write this more concisely as

```
max(x, y) => (x > y) ? x : y;
```

The first form uses an **if** statement, found in almost every programming language in similar form. The second form uses a conditional expression, common throughout the C family of languages. Using an expression allows us to use the short form of function declarations.

A more ambitious function is

```
maxElement(a) {
  var currentMax = a.isEmpty ?
    throw 'Maximal element undefined for empty array' : a[0];
  for (var i = 0; i < a.length; i++) {
    currentMax = max(a[i], currentMax);
  }
  return currentMax;
}
```

The function maxElement takes a list a and returns its largest element. Here we really need the long form of function declaration, because the computation will involve a number of steps that must be sequenced as a series of statements. This short function will illustrate a number of features of Dart.

The first line of the function body declares a variable named currentMax, and initializes it. Every variable in a Dart program must be explicitly declared. The variable currentMax represents our current estimate of the maximal element of the array.

In many languages, one might choose to initialize currentMax to a known value representing the smallest possible integer, typically denoted by a name like MIN_INT. Mathematically, the idea of "smallest possible integer" is absurd. However, in languages where integers are limited to a fixed size representation defined by the language, it makes sense. As noted above, Dart integers are not bounded in size, so instead we initialize currentMax to the first element of the list. If the list is empty, we can't do that, but then the argument a is invalid; the maximal element of an empty list is undefined. Consequently, we test to see if a is empty. If it is, we raise an exception, otherwise we choose the first element of the list as an initial candidate.

Exceptions are raised using a **throw** expression. The keyword **throw** is followed by another expression that defines the value to be thrown. In Dart, any kind of value can be thrown—it need not be a member of a special Exception type. In this case, we throw a string that describes the problem.

The next line begins a **for** statement that iterates through the list.[2] Every element is compared to currentMax in turn, by calling the max function defined earlier. If the current element is larger than currentMax, we set currentMax to the newly discovered maximal value.

After the loop is done, we are assured that currentMax is the largest element in the list and we return it.

Until now, this tutorial has carefully avoided any mention of terms like object, class or method. Dart allows you to define functions (such as twice, max and maxElement) and variables outside of any class. However, Dart is a thoroughly object-oriented language. All the values we've looked at — numbers, strings, Booleans, lists and even functions themselves are objects in Dart. Each such object is an instance of some class. Operations like length, isEmpty and even the indexing operator [] are all methods on objects.

It is high time we learned how to write a class ourselves. Behold the class Point, representing points in the cartesian plane:

```
class Point {
  var x, y;
  Point(a, b){x = a; y = b;}
}
```

The above is an extremely bare-bones version of Point which we will enrich shortly. A Point has two instance variables (or fields) x and y. We can create instances of Point by invoking its constructor via a **new** expression:

```
var origin = new Point(0, 0);
var aPoint = new Point(3, 4);
```

---

2. We start at index 0, but we could be slightly more efficient and start at 1 in this case.

```
var anotherPoint = new Point(3, 4);
```

Each of the three lines above allocates a fresh instance of Point, distinct from any other. In particular, aPoint and anotherPoint are different objects. An object has an identity, and that is what distinguishes it from any other object.

Each instance of Point has its own copies of the variables x and y, which can be accessed using the dot notation

```
origin.x // 0
origin.y // 0
aPoint.x // 3
aPoint.y // 4
```

The variables x and y are set by the constructor based on the actual parameters provided via **new**. The pattern of defining a constructor with formal parameters that correspond exactly to the fields of an object, and then setting those fields in the constructor, is very common, so Dart provides a special syntactic sugar for this case:

```
class Point {
  var x, y;
  Point(this.x, this.y);
}
```

The new version of Point is completely equivalent to the original, but more concise. Let's add some behavior to Point

```
class Point {
  var x, y;
  Point(this.x, this.y);
  scale(factor) => new Point(x * factor, y * factor);
}
```

This version has a method scale that takes a scaling factor factor as an argument and returns a new point, whose coordinates are based on the receiving point's, but scaled by factor.

```
aPoint.scale(2).x  // 6
anotherPoint.scale(10).y // 40
```

Another interesting operation on points is addition

```
class Point {
  var x, y;
  Point(this.x, this.y);
  scale(factor) => new Point(x * factor, y * factor);
  operator +(p) => new Point(x + p.x, y + p.y);
}
```

Now we can write expressions like

(aPoint + anotherPoint).y // 8

The operator + on points behaves just like an instance method; in fact, it is just an instance method with a strange name and a strange invocation syntax.

Dart also supports static members. We can add a static method inside of Point to compute the distance between two points:

```
static distance(p1, p2) {
  var dx = p1.x - p2.x;
  var dy = p1.y - p2.y;
  return sqrt(dx * dx + dy * dy);
}
```

The modifier **static** means this method is not specific to any instance. It has no access to the instance variables x and y, as those are different for each instance of Point. The method makes use of a library function, sqrt() that computes square roots. You might well ask, where does sqrt() come from? To understand that, we need to explain Dart's concept of modularity.

Dart code is organized into modular units called libraries. Each library defines its own namespace. The namespace includes the names of entities declared in the library. Additional names may be imported from other libraries. Declarations that are available to all Dart programs are defined in the Dart core library which is implicitly imported into all other Dart libraries. However, sqrt() is not one of them. It is defined in a library called dart:math, and if you want to use it, you must import it explicitly.

Here is a complete example of a library with an import, incorporating class Point

```
library points;

import 'dart:math';

class Point {
  var x, y;
  Point(this.x, this.y);
  scale(factor) => new Point(x * factor, y * factor);
  operator +(p) => new Point(x + p.x, y + p.y);
  static distance(p1, p2) {
    var dx = p1.x - p2.x;
    var dy = p1.y - p2.y;
    return sqrt(dx * dx + dy * dy);
  }
}
```

We have declared a library called points and imported the library dart:math. It is this import that makes sqrt available inside the points library. Now, any other library that wants to use our Point class can import points.

A key detail to note is that the **import** clause refers to a string 'dart:math'. In general, imports refer to uniform resource indicators (URIs) given via strings. The URIs point the compiler at a location where the desired library may be found. The built-in libraries of Dart are always available via URIs of the form 'dart:σ', where σ denotes a specific library.

There is a lot more to Dart than what we've shown so far, but you should have a general idea of what Dart code looks like and roughly what it means. This background will serve you well as we go into details later in the book.

1.5   Book Structure

The rest of the book is structured around the constructs of the Dart programming language. The next chapter discusses objects, classes and interfaces. These are the core concepts of Dart and are the foundation for all that follows.

Next, we examine libraries in detail, followed by a deeper look at functions. In Chapter 5, we finally take a look at types and the role they play in Dart. We review Dart's expressions and statements in Chapter 6. The final chapters investigate reflection and concurrency.

1.6   Related Work and Influences

The design of Dart has been influenced by earlier languages, in particular Smalltalk[1], Java and Javascript. Dart's syntax follows in the C tradition, via Java and Javascript. Dart's semantics are in some ways closer to Smalltalk - in particular, the insistence on a pure object model.

However, there are crucial differences. Dart introduces its own library-based encapsulation model. This differs from all three of the languages mentioned above. Smalltalk supports object-based encapsulation for fields, with methods and classes universally available. Java has a mix of class-based encapsulation and package privacy, and Javascript relies exclusively on closures for encapsulation.

Like Smalltalk and Java, Dart is class based and supports single inheritance, but it augments this with mixin-based inheritance, very similar to the model first implemented in the Strongtalk dialect of Smalltalk[2]. Because class methods in Dart are not true instance methods as in Smalltalk, but instead Java-style static methods, the models are not exactly the same.

Dart's constructors have a syntactic similarity to those of Java, but in fact differ in critical ways. All of the above topics are discussed in the next chapter.

Dart's approach to type checking is also very close to the one developed for Strongtalk. Types are explored exhaustively in Chapter 5.

Dart's view of concurrency is close to the original actor model (albeit, imperative), again very different from any of the languages cited above. The success of Erlang has been a factor in the adoption of an actor model, yet unlike Erlang, Dart has a non-blocking concurrency model. Dart also has built-in support for asynchrony heavily influenced by C#. See Chapter 8 for details.

Chapter 2

Objects, Interfaces, Classes and Mixins

It bears repeating: everything in Dart is an object. This includes even the simplest data such as numbers or the Boolean values **true** and **false**.

An object consists of a (possibly empty) set of fields, providing state, and a set of methods, providing behavior. The state of an object may be mutable or immutable. An object's set of methods is never empty because all Dart objects have some behavior. Objects get their behavior from their class. Every object has a class; we say that the object is *an instance of the class*. Because every object has a class that determines its behavior, Dart is a *class-based language*.

Consider the Point class we encountered in the previous chapter.

```
class Point {
  var x, y;
  Point(this.x, this.y);
  scale(factor) => new Point(x * factor, y * factor);
  operator +(p) => new Point(x + p.x, y + p.y);
  static distance(p1, p2) {
    var dx = p1.x - p2.x;
    var dy = p1.y - p2.y;
    return sqrt(dx * dx + dy * dy);
  }
}
```

Instances of Point each have two fields, x and y that constitute their state. Points also have several methods that provide useful behavior. These methods include scale and +, but there are in fact others. These additional methods are not defined by the class Point itself, but are *inherited* from its superclass. Every class has a superclass, except for the class Object which is built in to every Dart implementation. Classes may list their superclass explicitly, but do not have to. If a class does not list a superclass, the superclass is Object. This is the case with Point. We could have explicitly specified Object as the superclass of Point as follows; the two definitions are entirely equivalent.

```
class Point extends Object { ... rest of definition unchanged }
```

13

The methods that define an object's behavior are known as its *instance methods*. Note that the method distance() is not part of the behavior of instances of Point. It is a static method, not an instance method.

2.1 Accessors

Accessors are special methods that provide convenient access to values. To understand accessors, let us revisit Point once more, and consider how to change points so that they use a polar representation. We can easily replace the fields x and y with new fields rho and theta. However, we may have any number of clients that still require access to the Cartesian coordinates. So we might choose to compute these based upon the stored polar coordinates. The resulting class follows:

```
class Point {
  var rho, theta;
  Point(this.rho, this.theta);
  x() => rho * cos(theta);
  y() => rho * sin(theta);
  scale(factor) => new Point(rho * factor, theta);
  operator +(p) => new Point(x() + p.x(), y() + p.y());
  static distance(p1, p2) {
    var dx = p1.x() - p2.x();
    var dy = p1.y() - p2.y();
    return sqrt(dx * dx + dy * dy);
  }
}
```

The code is actually broken, because inside + we are calling the constructor with Cartesian coordinates whereas it expects polar coordinates. Set that issue aside; we'll deal with it later.[1]

The result is unsatisfactory for other reasons. We've replaced the fields x and y with methods to compute the corresponding values. All our clients are going to have to modify the references to x and y so that they are method invocations. For instance, if a client had a fragment such as

```
print(myPoint.x);
```

it needs to be changed to

```
print(myPoint.x());
```

The only difference is the empty argument list following x; it's a small change, but it is a change nevertheless. Modern tools can help, by automatically refactoring, but if one

---

1. Another issue we will ignore is the question of numerical precision; all these conversions may not yield perfect results.

modifies a widely used API, one does not know who all the clients are, and one cannot afford to burden them all with making such changes, even using convenient tools.

Dart provides a better solution in the form of *getter methods*, usually referred to as *getters*. A getter is a special method that takes no parameters, and can be called without an explicit argument list. A getter method is introduced by prefixing the method name with the word **get**. One must not give a parameter list—not even an empty one.

```
class Point {
  var rho, theta;
  Point(this.rho, this.theta);
  get x => rho * cos(theta);
  get y => rho * sin(theta);
  scale(factor) => new Point(rho * factor, theta);
  operator +(p) => new Point(x + p.x, y + p.y);
  static distance(p1, p2) {
    var dx = p1.x - p2.x;
    var dy = p1.y - p2.y;
    return sqrt(dx * dx + dy * dy);
  }
}
```

Now our hypothetical clients need not be changed. The syntax for a getter invocation is indistinguishable from a variable access.

The alert reader should now ask how does the Dart compiler know the difference between the two? The answer is that it doesn't. All instance variable accesses in Dart are actually getter calls. An instance variable always has a getter associated with it, courtesy of the Dart compiler.

So far we've only solved part of the problem. What about clients that assign to the fields, such as

```
myPoint.y = myPoint.y * 2.
```

The new version has no field that can be assigned. It isn't clear what change the client can make to keep their code running. To address this issue we use *setter methods* (*setters* for short). A setter is prefixed with the word **set** and takes a single parameter. A setter is invoked using the same syntax as a conventional variable assignment. If an instance variable is mutable, a setter is automatically defined for it, and all instance variable assignments are in fact setter calls.

```
class Point {
  var rho, theta;
  Point(this.rho, this.theta);
  get x => rho * cos(theta);
  set x(newX) {
    rho = sqrt(newX * newX + y * y);
```

```
      theta = acos(newX/rho);
   }
   set y(newY) {
      rho = sqrt(x * x + newY * newY);
      theta = asin(newY/rho);
   }
   get y => rho * sin(theta);
   scale(factor) => new Point(rho * factor, theta);
   operator +(p) => new Point(x + p.x, y + p.y);
   static distance(p1, p2) {
      var dx = p1.x() - p2.x();
      var dy = p1.y() - p2.y();
      return sqrt(dx * dx + dy * dy);
   }
}
```

At this point, we've solved two parts of the problem, but there remains a third part. Our clients created points by invoking the constructor of class Point, as in

```
new Point(3,4);
```

Our new class expects the arguments to the constructor to represent the length and orientation of the vector, not its Cartesian coordinates. And as we noted earlier, we rely on this API inside the class as well, and so there is no way that this will function correctly. As usual, the solution is to preserve the existing API while still changing the representation as desired. We therefore choose to use the polar representation, but to maintain the interface, we retain the existing constructor which takes Cartesian arguments.

```
class Point {
   var rho, theta;
   Point(a, b){
      rho = sqrt(a * a + b * b);
      theta = atan(a/b);
   }
   ... rest unchanged ...
}
```

We have now achieved our goal of changing the representation of points without any impact on their clients. We did this without any pre-planning. We did not have to decide in advance to expose the coordinates of points via accessor methods or special property declarations; Dart did that for us, without any syntactic inconvenience. We could have fixed the constructor in any mainstream language. However, without accessors, a completely smooth transition would not have been possible.

2.2 Instance Variables

When a class declares an instance variable, it is ensuring that each of its instances will have its own unique copy of the variable. The instance variables of an object occupy memory. This memory is allocated when an object is created. It's important that this memory be set to some reasonable value before the program can access it. In low-level languages such as C, this is not necessarily the case, and the contents of freshly allocated storage may be undefined—typically whatever value was stored in them before. This causes problems with respect to reliability and security.

Dart initializes every newly allocated variable (not just instance variables, but also local variables, class variables and top-level variables) to **null**. In Dart, **null** is an object, much like any other. One must not confuse **null** with other objects such as 0 or **false**. The object **null** is simply the unique instance of the class Null defined in the Dart core library. This is different from the situation in languages such as C, C++, C#, Java or Javascript, but is an inevitable consequence of the axiom that everything is an object.

Declaring an instance or static variable automatically introduces a getter. If the variable is mutable, a setter is also automatically defined. In fact, fields are never accessed directly in Dart. All references to fields are invocations of accessor methods. Only the accessors of an object may directly access its state. All code that accesses an object's state has to go through these accessor methods. This means that the representation of a class can be always be changed without any change to client source code. Even recompilation is not required—ever! This property is known as *representation independence*.

We saw the advantage of representation independence in the previous section, where we showed how to change the representation of points without modifying any code that used points.

2.3 Class Variables

In addition to instance variables, classes may define *class variables*. A class has only one copy of a class variable, regardless of how many instances it has. The variable exists even if there are no instances at all.

A class variable declaration is prefaced with the word **static**. We could add a class variable to a class to track how many instances have been created.

```
class Box {
  static var numberOfInstances = 0;
  Box(){numberOfInstances = numberOfInstances + 1;}
}
```

Here, every time the constructor of class Box() runs, it increments the count of all boxes ever made.

Like instance variables, class variables are never referenced directly. All accesses to them are mediated via accessors.

A class variable can be referred to by its name anywhere within its declaring class. Outside the class, it can be accessed only by prefixing it with the name of the class that declared it:

```
Box.numberOfInstances == 0 ? print('No boxes yet') : print('We have boxes!');
```

Class variables are often referred to as static variables, but the term "static variable" is also used to encompass both class variables and top-level variables. To avoid any confusion, we'll stick with the term "class variable." We will often use the term "fields" when we speak of instance and class variables collectively.

Class variables are initialized lazily; the initializer of a class variable is executed the first time its getter is invoked—that is, the first time one attempts to read the variable. If a class variable has no initializer, it is initialized to **null**, just like any other variable.

Lazy initialization of class variables helps avoid a classic problem: sluggish application startup due to an excess of up-front initialization. However, laziness can cause surprising behavior. Suppose a class variable is assigned before it has been read, as in the example below.

```
class Cat {}
class DeadCat extends Cat {}
class LiveCat extends Cat {
  LiveCat() {print("I'm alive!");}
}
var schrodingers = new LiveCat();

main() {
  schrodingers = new DeadCat();
}
```

Here, the initializer of schrodingers will never be executed, and the call to print() will never be executed. While this may seem pretty obvious above, in more complex situations that may not be the case. For example, during debugging one might check for the variable's value, which would provoke initialization. Programmers should always pay close attention to the implications of lazy initialization.

2.4 Finals

Variables in Dart may be prefixed with the word **final**, indicating that they may not be changed after they are initialized. A final field has a getter but no setter. Final class variables must be initialized at the point they are declared.

Final instance variables must be initialized before any instance methods are run. There are several ways of accomplishing this. The first is to initialize the variable at its point of declaration, for example,

```
final origin = new Point(0,0);
```

This isn't always convenient. It may be that the variable will be set differently in different constructors. For example it may depend on the arguments to the constructor. If one wants the value of a final instance variable to be set to the value of a constructor argument, one can use the common constructor shorthand. As an example, consider this variant of Point where points are immutable:

```
class Point {
  final x, y;
  Point(this.x, this.y);
  // the rest of Point ...
}
```

However, sometimes this is not enough. The value may depend on a constructor argument, but be different—that is, it may involve some computation based on the constructor argument. We'll look into how to achieve this in just a little while, in section 2.9

Attempting to assign a final instance variable will usually lead to a NoSuchMethodError, since an assignment is just sugar for invoking a setter, and the setter won't be defined. It is possible that a setter was declared separately however, in which case it will get invoked. This won't have any effect on the value of the instance variable however—there is simply no way to change a final variable after it is initialized.

Most instance variables are set when the instance is allocated and never change afterwards. You might find this surprising, but this has been verified by systematic studies[3]. It is therefore best to declare most instance variables **final**.

There is a strong argument that **final** should be the default, but that runs against established habit, and so Dart makes the traditional choice here.

2.5   Identity and Equality

All objects support the equality operator ==. This operator is defined in class Object, so all classes inherit it, and it is thus included in the behavior of all instances. Consider

```
var aPoint = new Point(3, 4);
var anotherPoint = new Point(3,4);
aPoint == anotherPoint; // evaluates to false
```

The result of the last line is somewhat disturbing. After all, both aPoint and anotherPoint have the same x and y values, so why are they not equal?

The method == in Object tests whether the argument is identical to the receiver. As noted earlier, each object has a unique identity. An object is identical to itself, and only to itself. Two objects can be instances of the same class and have the exact same state, yet still not be identical, as the above example shows.

The above explanation is rather mechanistic. We say that the two objects are not equal because equality is defined as identity, but this begs the question of why equality is defined this way.

Unfortunately, there is no obviously correct way to decide if two arbitrary objects are equal. One could compare all the fields of the object for equality, but this is still too conservative. An object may have fields that are used to store auxiliary data that is not essential to the semantics of equality. For example, suppose we have a timestamp that tells us when some cached value was last computed. The cache is considered stale after some time. Two objects might differ on the timestamp (or on the cached value) and yet still be equal.

And so, it is the responsibility of the programmer who defines a class to determine what notion of equality makes sense for instances of the class. The way to do this is to override ==.[2] In the case of Point we can define equality as

```
operator == (p) => x == p.x && y == p.y;
```

Notice that this code remains valid (modulo issues of numeric precision) even if we switch to polar coordinates (though it may not be as efficient). In fact, it holds even if p is a Cartesian point and the receiver is polar, or any other combination.

There are situations where one may wish to check if two expressions denote identical objects, but they are relatively rare. Typically, one tests objects for equality.

One can compare the identities of two objects using the built in function identical(), defined in dart:core.

We find that identical(origin, origin) evaluates to **true**, as do identical(aPoint, aPoint) and identical(anotherPoint, anotherPoint). On the other hand identical(aPoint, another-Point) evaluates to **false**.

We now know enough to define the equality method of class Object ourselves:

```
bool operator ==(other) => identical(this, other);
```

All Dart objects also support the getter method hashCode. Equality and hashCode are interrelated. If two objects are equal, their hash codes should be equal. Implementors must take care to preserve this property. In practice, this means that if you choose to override either one of these methods, you should override the other as well.

Implementing user-defined equality requires some care. We expect our equality predicates to be reflexive (a == a), transitive ((a == b) && (b == c) implies a == c) and commutative (a == b implies b == a). Reflexivity is something you can ensure in your own implementation of ==. The other properties are difficult to preserve in an extensible system. One can always introduce

```
class BadApple {
  operator == (x) => true;
}
```

and undermine the mathematical properties of equality throughout the system.

---

2. It would be nice to use = for equality, but the C tradition and mathematics contradict each other.

2.6 Class and Superclass

Each class declares a set of instance members that include instance variables and several kinds of instance methods. In addition, every class (except Object) inherits instance members from its superclass. Since every class except Object has exactly one superclass, and Object has no superclass, the Dart class hierarchy forms a tree with Object as its root. This arrangement is known as *single inheritance*, and is illustrated below.

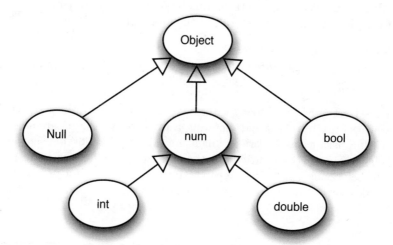

In the diagram, we see the class hierarchy for numbers, Booleans and Null. Of course, this is just a small fragment of the entire Dart class hierarchy.

If a subclass declares an instance method with the same name as a method of its superclass, the subclass method is said to *override* the superclass method.

Overrides are not always legal. You can't override a getter with an ordinary method or vice versa for example. These situations will lead to a compilation error.

```
class S {
    var v;
    final f = 0;
    get g => 42;
    set s(x) => v = 2;
    m(a, b) => 91;
}

class C extends S {
    v() => 1; // ILLEGAL: method v() overrides implicit getter method v
    f() => 2; // ILLEGAL: method f() overrides implicit getter method f
    g() => 100; // ILLEGAL: method g() overrides getter method g
}
```

Attempting to override a setter with a method or getter, or to override a method or getter with a setter is technically impossible because the names of setters do not overlap with those of methods and getters. However, Dart will warn you if you try:

```
class D extends S {
  s(y) => 200; // WARNING: D has method s and setter s=
}
```

There are cases where a nonsensical override will result in a warning rather than a compilation error. When an overriding method requires more parameters than the method it overrides a warning is issued but the program will still compile.

```
class E extends S {
  m(x, y, z) => 101; // WARNING: overriding method has incompatible arity
}
```

Why does Dart only warn about this situation rather than reject the code out of hand? Because Dart tries to avoid dictating a workflow to the programmer as much as possible. Inconsistencies of various kinds can arise during development and should ultimately be corrected. However, forcing the programmer to deal with these situations immediately, before any other progress can be made is often counter-productive. Therefore Dart makes sure that the developer is alerted to such problems via warnings, but does not abort compilation unless it is absolutely essential.

2.7   Abstract Methods and Classes

Often it is useful to simply declare a method without providing its implementation. Such a method is called an *abstract method*. Any kind of instance method can be abstract, regardless of whether it is a getter, setter, operator or ordinary method.

Declaring an abstract method tells anyone reading the code (human or computer) that such a method is expected to be available when code is actually executed. This improves programmer comprehension as well as error handling and tooling.

A class that has an abstract method is itself an *abstract class*. Abstract classes are declared by prefacing their declaration with the word **abstract**.

Below we see an abstract class Pair that contains no implementation information whatsoever. It acts purely as an interface, as we'll describe below.

```
abstract class Pair {
  get first;
  get second;
}
```

Pair has two abstract getter methods, first and second. Pair is explicitly declared as an abstract class. If we omitted the **abstract** modifier, the Dart analyzer would issue a warning that the class has abstract methods. It is of course perfectly correct to have abstract methods in an abstract class, but it is clearly a problem to retain such methods in a concrete class. The **abstract** modifier allows us to declare our intent and the warnings the analyzer issues will vary accordingly.

An abstract class is not intended to be instantiated; after all, it is missing parts of its implementation. Instantiating it will result in a runtime error; specifically, an AbstractClassInstantiationError will be raised. The Dart analyzer would issue a warning as well.

```
new Pair();
// Static warning: attempting to instantiate an abstract class
// Throws an AbstractClassInstantiationError
```

As far as the runtime is concerned, an abstract method simply doesn't exist. After all, there is no implementation to run. Invoking such a method is treated exactly the same as if no method declaration were present.

A class that only contains abstract methods is useful in defining interfaces, as described in the next section.

2.8 Interfaces

Every class implicitly defines an *interface* that describes what methods are available on its instances. Dart does not have formal interface declarations like those found in many other languages. These are unnecessary, as one can always define an abstract class to describe a desired interface.

```
abstract class CartesianPoint {
  get x;
  get y;
}
```

```
abstract class PolarPoint {
  get rho;
  get theta;
}
```

Despite the absence of interface declarations, classes may assert that their instances implement specific interfaces

```
class Point implements CartesianPoint, PolarPoint {
// Usual Point implementation goes here
}
```

Point is not a subclass of CartesianPoint; it does not inherit any members from CartesianPoint (or PolarPoint for that matter). The purpose of the **implements** clause is to establish an intended relationship between interfaces, not to share implementations.

It is possible to test whether an object conforms to an interface at runtime:

```
5 is int; // true
'x' is String; // true
[] is Point; // false
aPoint.toString() is String; // true
new Point(0,0) is String; // false
aPoint is CartesianPoint; // true
```

Note that an **is** test does not check whether the object is actually an instance of a given class or one of its subclasses. Rather, the **is** test checks whether an object's class explicitly implements an interface (directly or indirectly). In other words, we are not concerned about what the implementation of an object is, but only with the interface it is intended to support. This is a crucial difference compared to most other languages that support such constructs. If a class wishes to emulate the interface of another class, it is not constrained to share implementation. Such emulation should be indistinguishable (modulo reflection(7)) to clients. We'll have more to say about **is** in Chapter 5 when we examine types in detail.

Interfaces inherit from each other very much like classes do. The implicit interface of a class inherits from the implicit interface of its superclass as well as from any interfaces the class implements. As with classes, instance methods of an interface override those from superinterfaces. Again, some overrides may be illegal because the number of arguments should be compatible between the overriding method and the overridden one, or because one is trying to override a getter or setter with an ordinary method or vice versa.

Additionally, because an interface has multiple direct superinterfaces, conflicts can arise between the different superinterfaces. Assume a method occurs in more than one superinterface, and the different superinterfaces have versions of the same method that disagree on the method arity. In this situation, no version of the conflicting method is inherited — likewise if one superinterface defines a getter and another an ordinary method. As we'll see in Chapter 5, these situations will give rise to various warnings as well.

2.9   Life of an Object

Computation in Dart revolves around objects. Because Dart is a purely object-oriented language, even the most trivial Dart program involves the creation of objects. For example, the "Hello World" program shown in the very first paragraph of the book involves the creation of a string object.

Some objects, such as the string 'Hello World', the Boolean value **true** or the number 91 are *literals*. These come in to being simply by virtue of being mentioned in a running program. Most objects, however, are created explicitly using an instance creation expression such as **new** Point(0,1). Such an expression calls a *constructor*—in this case, Point(). Every class has at least one constructor. The name of a constructor always begins with the name of the class whose instance we want to construct. Constructors may be declared explicitly by the programmer, or they may be generated implicitly. Implicit constructors are generated when no explicit constructor is declared; they take no arguments and have no body. For example

```
class Box {
  var contents;
}
```

is equivalent to

```
class Box {
  var contents;
  Box();
}
```

which itself is equivalent to

```
class Box {
  var contents;
  Box(){}
}
```

We have already seen a few variations of constructors in our examples using Point. We'll assume the simplest one:

```
Point(a, b){x = a; y = b;};
```

The first step in evaluating an instance creation expression is evaluating the arguments to the constructor. In **new** Point(0,1), the arguments are the literal integers 0 and 1. As with any function invocation, the parameters are set to the corresponding arguments. So we have a set to 0 and b set to 1. Now we can allocate a fresh instance of class Point, which will have storage for two fields, x and y. Initially, these fields will be set to null by the system. This ensures that user code will never encounter uninitialized memory.

We can now execute the body of the constructor, which involves two assignments, to x and y respectively. As you know by now, these assignments are really setter method invocations. It is the implicitly defined setters that actually set the values of the fields x and y to 0 and 1 as expected. At this point, the constructor returns a reference to the newly allocated instance, which is the end result of the **new** expression.

Now, let us consider a class representing three-dimensional points. This class has coordinates x, y and z and can naturally be declared as a subclass of Point.

```
class Point3D extends Point {
  var z;
  Point3D(a, b, c): super(a,b) {z = c;}
}
```

One can create an instance of Point3D by writing **new** Point3D(1,2,3). The evaluation process is similar but a little more involved. We still begin by evaluating the arguments and allocating the object—this time with three fields—the two inherited fields x, y from Point, and the z field declared in Point3D. All three fields will again be set to null. However, before executing the body of the Point3D constructor, we will have to execute the body of the Point constructor, otherwise the fields x and y will not be properly initialized.

In general, the Dart compiler cannot determine what arguments should be passed to the super constructor. It may seem obvious in this case, but it is not always so simple. In all but the simplest cases (where there are no arguments) we require an explicit *super-constructor call* to guide us. In our example, that is **super**(a,b). In a superconstructor call, **super** is a stand-in for the name of the superclass, so that Point3D(x1, y1, z1) calls Point(x1, y1) before executing its own body.

The description above is a bit simplistic, as we will see shortly. Object creation is one of the more involved aspects of object-oriented programming languages, especially in the face of inheritance. To refine our understanding further, we shall look once more at the question of changing the representation of points. This time, assume that points are immutable, but are represented using polar coordinates.

Since the points are immutable, rho and theta are **final**. We cannot initialize the instance variables at their declaration, since we need access to the constructor arguments. We cannot use initializing formals like **this**.rho, since the values of rho and theta are each a function of both x and y. And we cannot assign the fields inside the constructor body, because no setter is defined for them. Dart solves this problem with *initializer lists*, which are designed to initialize instance variables before ordinary code is run.

```
class Point {
  final rho, theta;
  Point(a, b) :  rho = sqrt(a * a + b * b), theta = atan(a/b);
  get x => rho * cos(theta);
  get y => rho * sin(theta);
  scale(factor) => new Point(rho * factor, theta);
  operator +(p) => new Point(x + p.x, y + p.y);
  static distance(p1, p2) {
    var dx = p1.x - p2.x;
    var dy = p1.y - p2.y;
    return sqrt(dx * dx + dy * dy);
  }
}
```

The initializer list here starts with the colon following Point(a, b) and continues until the semicolon at the end of the line: : rho = sqrt(a * a + b * b), theta = atan(a/b). It consists of two initializers, one for rho and one for theta. Initializers are separated by commas and are executed from left to right. Besides initializers for instance variables, an initializer list may contain a single superconstructor call. We saw this in Point3D(), where we had the initializer list : **super**(a,b). Note that if no superconstructor call appears in the initializer list explicitly, an implicit super constructor call of the form **super**() is appended to the list.

We have seen several ways to initialize instance variables. Let's review them again. One can initialize an instance variable at its point of declaration

```
class Point {
  var x = 0, y = 0;
}
```

or via initializing formals in a constructor

```
class Point {
  var x, y;
  Point(this.x, this.y);
}
```

or in an initializer list

```
class Point {
  var x, y;
  Point(a, b) : x = a, y = b;
}
```

or in a constructor body

```
class Point {
  var x, y;
  Point(a, b) { x = a;  y = b;}
}
```

For an ordinary instance variable, one can choose any one of these options, or several of them, or none at all. The last option is not available for final instance variables because it uses setter methods, which finals do not have. Final instance variables must be initialized only once, and so one has to choose one of the first three options above.

When an object is instantiated, the various initialization constructs are executed in the order listed above.

We can now describe the process of instance creation in its full glory. Assume that Point3D is defined as above, and that Point has the following constructor:

Point(a, b) : x = a, y = b;

The instance creation process is illustrated below, with execution following the direction of the arrow:

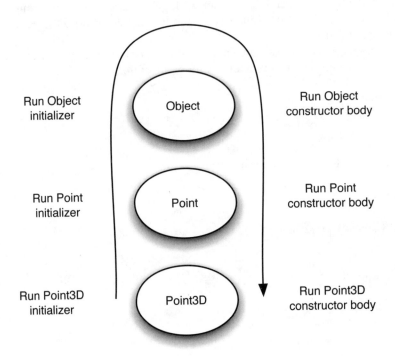

Run Object initializer — Object — Run Object constructor body

Run Point initializer — Point — Run Point constructor body

Run Point3D initializer — Point3D — Run Point3D constructor body

Creating a new instance of Point3D via **new** Point3D(7, 8, 9) begins by computing the actual arguments, which in this case are 7, 8 and 9. Then the constructor Point3D() is called. The next step is allocating a fresh instance of Point3D. All instance variables are set to null. We then proceed to execute the initializer list of Point3D. This causes the super initializer to be executed, which causes the initializer list of Point to be executed. This will set the instance variables x and y, and then execute the implicit super initializer added at the end of Point's initializer list. This will call the initializer list of Object which does nothing (it doesn't even have a super initializer at the end). All these steps are shown on the left side of the figure above.

Having completed traversing all the initializer lists in the superclass chain, the next step is to execute the constructor body. In the figure, this corresponds to the u-turn of the arrow.

A constructor body always begins by implicitly running the superconstructor body. The arguments passed to the superconstructor are the same ones used in the superconstructor call given in the initializer list. They are not recomputed. So in our case, we'll start running the body of Point3D(), which starts running the body of Point(), which starts running the body of Object(), which does nothing. Since no body was specified for Point(), we return to the body of Point3D() where we initialize z, after which we return the newly allocated object. The process corresponds to the right side of our diagram.

2.9.1 Redirecting Constructors

Sometimes it is useful to define a constructor in terms of another. Consider the case
of converting from Cartesian points to polar points again. Our previous effort only
allowed points to be created from Cartesian coordinates. Given the fact that our actual
representation was polar, this is a bit odd. Of course, we could just change the constructor to take polar coordinates, but we know that is problematic because we have
existing users who depend on the Cartesian interface. We really should retain the old
constructor, but also add a new one that accepts polar coordinates. We'll define a new
named constructor Point.polar() for this purpose, and revise the pre-existing constructor
so that it converts incoming Cartesian coordinates into polar ones, and forwards the
call to Point.polar().

```
class Point {
  var rho, theta;
  Point.polar(this.rho, this.theta);
  Point(a, b) : this.polar( sqrt(a * a + b * b), atan(a/b));
  get x => rho * cos(theta);
  set x(newX) {
    rho = sqrt(newX * newX + y * y);
    theta = acos(newX/rho);
  }
  set y(newY) {
    rho = sqrt(x * x + newY * newY);
    theta = asin(newY/rho);
  }
  get y => rho * sin(theta);
  scale(factor) => new Point.polar(rho * factor, theta);
  operator +(p) => new Point(x + p.x, y + p.y);
  static distance(p1, p2) {
    var dx = p1.x - p2.x;
    var dy = p1.y - p2.y;
    return sqrt(dx * dx + dy * dy);
  }
}
```

Point() is now a *redirecting constructor*. The purpose of a redirecting constructor is, as you might guess, to redirect execution to another constructor, in this case
Point.polar(). In a redirecting constructor, the parameter list is followed by a colon and
a call of the form **this**.*id*(...) which specifies which constructor to redirect to.

At this point, we have successfully converted the representation of points while
preserving the original API of the class. We've used a named constructor Point.polar() to
manufacture points using the new representation, allowing us to keep the old constructor
in place. We converted the old constructor into a redirecting constructor so that it

produces our revised points. We also used getters and setters to preserve the original API of point instances.

2.9.2   Factories

Now suppose we want to avoid excess allocation of points. Rather than generating a fresh point on every request, we'd like to maintain a cache of points. Whenever someone tries to allocate a point, we'd like to check our cache and see if an equivalent point is already there, and return that one.

Traditionally, constructors make that difficult. In most languages, a constructor always allocates a fresh instance as we've described. If you want to use a cache, you need to think of this in advance, and ensure that your points are allocated via a method call, often referred to as a factory method.

Tragically, programmers are denied the gift of perfect foresight, and on occasion may fail to predict the need for a cache in advance. In Dart however, any constructor may be replaced with a factory in a manner that is completely transparent to the client. We do this by means of *factory constructors*.

Factory constructors are prefaced by the word **factory**. They look like ordinary constructors, except that they may not have initializer lists or initializing formal parameters. Instead, they must have a body that returns an object. The factory can return the object from a cache, or it can allocate a fresh instance as it chooses. It can even allocate instances of a different class (or look them up in a cache or any other data structure). As long as the resulting object complies with the interface of the class, all will be well.

In this way, Dart addresses some of the classic weaknesses of traditional constructors.

2.10   noSuchMethod()

Computation in Dart revolves around calling methods on objects. If one calls a method that doesn't exist, the default behavior is to raise a NoSuchMethodError. However, this is not always the case.

When one calls a method that doesn't exist on an instance, the Dart runtime calls the method noSuchMethod() on that same object. Because the implementation of noSuch-Method() in Object throws NoSuchMethodError, we usually see the familiar behavior.

The beauty of this scheme is that noSuchMethod() can be overridden. For example, if you are implementing a proxy for another object, you can define the proxy's noSuchMethod() to forward all invocations to the target of the proxy.

```
class Proxy {
  final forwardee;
  Proxy(this.forwardee);
  noSuchMethod(inv) { return runMethod(forwardee, inv);}
}
```

The argument to noSuchMethod() is an instance of Invocation, a special type defined in the core library and used to describe method invocations. An Invocation reflects the original call, describing what was the name of the method we were trying to invoke, what were the arguments, and a few other details.

In order to actually forward each call to forwardee, our implementation of noSuch-Method() makes use of an auxiliary function runMethod() that takes a receiver object and an invocation, and invokes the named method on the receiver with the arguments supplied. We'll show how to implement runMethod() later, when we discuss reflection in Chapter 7.

A robust implementation of a proxy is a little bit more involved than the code above. One subtlety is that Proxy will not forward methods defined in Object, since these are inherited and will not cause noSuchMethod() to be called. The interface of Object is small by design and can be intercepted manually.

Even with these complications, a full implementation of Proxy is straightforward. Later in the book, once we've learned a few more tricks, we'll show a full version of Proxy. The ability to code a general-purpose proxy, independent of the type of the target, is a perfect example of the flexibility an optionally typed language like Dart can provide. Such flexibility is missing in mandatory typed languages.

We shall see several interesting additional uses of noSuchMethod() throughout this book.

2.11 Constant Objects and Fields

Some objects are constants that can be computed at compile-time. Many of these are obvious: literal numbers like 3.14159, literal strings like 'Hello World' and so forth. We will give a detailed account of constant expressions in section 6.1.4.

Dart also supports user-defined constant objects, and these will be our focus here. Let's see if we can make constant points

```
class Point {
  final x, y;
  const Point(this.x, this.y);
  ... the usual
}
const origin = const Point(0,0);
```

Under the right conditions we can produce a constant Point object representing the origin. The origin variable is declared to be a constant. We can only assign a constant object to it. Constant objects get created using **const** instead of **new**. Like a **new** expression, a **const** expression invokes a constructor, but that constructor must be a constant constructor, and the arguments to the constructor must themselves be constant. In fact, Dart requires that the arguments also be restricted to numbers, Booleans or strings. Fortunately, numeric literals like 0 are always constants.

We've declared Point's constructor to be constant. That imposes some pretty severe restrictions on the class and on the constructor itself. We need a class whose state is immutable. Fortunately, immutable points are quite natural.

In addition, a constant constructor cannot have a body. It can have an initializer list, provided that it only computes constants (assuming that the parameters are known constants). In our case, no computation is required.

Unfortunately, we could not define a constructor like Point.polar() as a constant constructor, since it makes use of functions like sqrt() whose results are not considered constant. It's okay for Point to have such a constructor—we just can't invoke it using **const**. So any points we'd create with this constructor would not be constants.

We don't have to create constant points all the time. In fact, we can still call a constant constructor using **new**. If we do that, there are no restrictions on the arguments we pass, but the results will not be constants.

Constants can be computed in advance, once, and need not be recomputed. Constants are canonicalized—only one constant of a given value is ever created in a Dart program.

2.12   Class Methods

Class methods are methods that are not tied to individual instances. We've already encountered some of these when discussing class variables. The accessors induced by class variables are class methods. We may speak of class getters or class setters. Besides the automatically induced class accessors, programmers can define such accessors explicitly. Indeed, one can define ordinary methods on a per-class basis as well.

We saw such an example in Chapter 1. In class Point we had

```
static distance(p1, p2) {
   var dx = p1.x() - p2.x();
   var dy = p1.y() - p2.y();
   return sqrt(dx * dx + dy * dy);
}
```

Just like class variable accessors, the names of user-defined class methods are available within the class that declares them. Outside the class, the methods can only be accessed if they are prefixed with the name of their enclosing class, for example, Point.distance(aPoint, anotherPoint).

It is a compilation error to use **this** inside a class method. Since a class method is not specific to any instance, **this** is not defined within it.

If you try and call a class method that doesn't exist, you'll get a runtime error:

```
Point.distant(aPoint, anotherPoint); // NoSuchMethodError!
```

This behavior highlights an interesting design issue. Since this is a static call, the Dart compiler can detect, at compile-time, that there is no class method distant() in Point. Why not give a compilation error on the spot? After all, we know for a fact that this code must fail at runtime.

However, Dart is designed to keep out of the programmer's way as much as possible. During development, incomplete fragments of code may be written and tested in a spirit of experimentation. A programmer may prefer to test one path through the code, knowing full well that another path is not yet functional.

In systems that insist on complete definitions developers work around such requirements by defining stubs. These stubs will lead to incorrect results or failure at runtime, and their only purpose is to allow development to move forward by silencing an overzealous compiler.

Of course, the compiler's zeal is not entirely unmotivated. The undefined method might just as easily be a typographical error:

```
Pont.distance(aPoint, anotherPoint); // NoSuchMethodError!
```

The difference between the undefined class Pont and the intended class Point can be very hard for a human to detect and the programmer may spend a long, frustrating time trying to understand the cause of the failure. Worse, the failure may not be on a tested code path, resulting in a crash in production.

Fortunately, Dart will give a static warning in these cases, but still compile and run the code. This provides the flexibility of a dynamic system with much of the assurance provided by a conventional type system.

It's important to remember that class members are never inherited

```
class ExtendedPoint extends Point {
  var origin = new Point(0,0);
  get distanceFromOrigin => distance(origin, this);
  // sorry, NoSuchMethodError!
}
```

The getter method distanceFromOrigin cannot make use of the name distance. We could have defined distanceFromOrigin in Point itself (assuming we also defined origin) but distance is not in scope in any subclass of Point. To make this work, we'd have to write

```
get distanceFromOrigin => Point.distance(origin, this); // ok
```

Since class methods are never inherited, it makes no sense to declare an abstract class method. You won't get far if you try, as it is not even syntactically valid.

2.13 Instances, Their Classes and Metaclasses

Every object is an instance of a class. Since everything is an object, classes are objects too, and since classes are objects, they are themselves instances of a class. The class of a class is often referred to as a *metaclass*. The Dart language mandates that classes have type Type, but does not specify what class they belong to.

In a typical implementation, the classes might be instances of a private class _Type. What would the class of _Type be? Usually it would be _Type—that is, _Type would be an instance of itself, resolving what might otherwise be an infinite regress. The situation is illustrated in the following diagram, showing an object aC which is an instance of a class C which is an instance of _Type, which is an instance of itself.

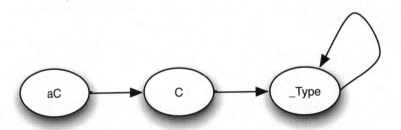

The only way to reliably discover what the class of an object is is via reflection, which we will discuss extensively in Chapter 7. Objects do support a getter runtimeType, which by default does return the class of the object. However, subclasses are free to override runtimeType.

It is important that one can override runtimeType. Recall our Proxy example above. The proxy object must be indistinguishable from the real objects. If runtimeType was hardwired, we could find out that these proxies were instances of Proxy.

More generally, the principle that the only thing that matters about an object is its behavior can all too easily be violated. It requires great care to ensure that nothing in the language causes irrelevant implementation details of this nature to leak.

On the other hand, some code might have a legitimate need to find out the actual class of an object. An IDE, or debugger, or a profiler is expected to show true and accurate information. The mechanism for this is reflection.

Finally, a rather disturbing anomaly. It is too easy to confuse calling class methods with invoking instance methods on type literals

```
Type.runtimeType; // Ouch! NoSuchMethodError
(Type).runtimeType; // works
```

The first line is a call to a non-existent class method; the class Type does not have a class method runtimeType. The second invokes the method runtimeType defined for all objects on the type literal Type. We could resolve this issue by viewing class methods as instance methods on the corresponding Type object but this not the case at the moment.

2.14   Object and Its Methods

The interface of class Object is exceedingly small. We have in fact encountered almost all of its methods. We encountered the operator method == along with the getter hashCode in section 2.5. Section 2.10 revolved around noSuchMethod(). We saw runtimeType in the immediately preceding section. And perhaps the most commonly used method of all is toString(). This method returns a string representing the object. The default version will typically print out something like 'An Instance of C' where C is the name of the class of the object. It's often useful override it to something more meaningful.

Altogether, only five methods constitute the interface shared by all objects. An outline of class Object would look like this

```
class Object {
  bool operator == (another) { ... }
  int get hashCode { ... }
  String toString(){ ... }
  noSuchMethod(Invocation im) { ... }
  Type get runtimeType{ ... }
}
```

You'll notice that, for the first time, types have made their appearance in our code. Dart code may be decorated with type annotations, and the Dart core libraries almost always are. As you might expect, equality yields a Boolean result, the hash code is an integer, toString() returns a string and the runtime type is, well, a Type. As discussed above, noSuchMethod() takes an Invocation. The syntax should be familiar to most programmers.

We've elided the bodies of the methods. In fact, if you look at the source code you'll find something close, yet different:

```
class Object {
  bool operator == (other)=>  identical(this, other);
  external int get hashCode;
  external String toString();
  external noSuchMethod(Invocation im);
  external Type get runtimeType;
}
```

Except for == whose implementation we figured out earlier, all the other methods are supplied by the Dart implementation rather than implemented directly in Dart code. They are marked as **external** indicating that their implementation is being provided elsewhere. The **external** mechanism is useful for declaring code whose implementation comes from the outside. There are various ways such code can be provided—via a foreign function interface, as primitives of the underlying implementation (as is the case here) or possibly even dynamically generated implementations. The first of these scenarios is by far the most likely one for most programmers.

2.15   Mixins

Sometimes single inheritance can be rather constraining. A classic real-life example comes when implementing GUI frameworks. You find that you need a compound widget that groups together several smaller widgets. It is very natural and convenient to view this compound widget as a collection. Collections have some useful shared functionality, so you'd like to define CompoundWidget to inherit from Collection. There's only one catch; you also want CompoundWidget to inherit from Widget, since it is a widget and there is a lot of useful functionality to be had there as well.

One approach has been to allow a class to have multiple superclasses. Experience has shown this to be more trouble than it is worth. Instead, Dart uses *mixin-based inheritance.*

To understand mixin-based inheritance, we shall examine a simplified collection class

```
abstract class Collection {
    forEach(f); // perform the function f on each element of the collection
    where(f) ...
    map(f) ...
}
```

What we really want from Collection is its body—the stuff between the curly braces. The body contains the functionality the class declaration itself contributes. It is the difference between a Collection and its superclass. We call this difference a *mixin.*

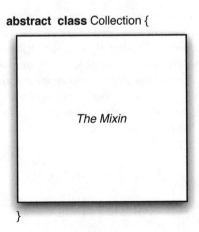

abstract class Collection {

The Mixin

}

We'd like to take this functionality and "mix it in" to CompoundWidget as illustrated below.

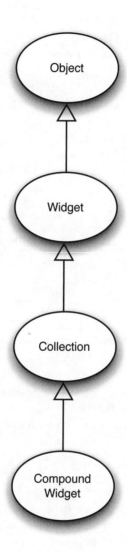

We could achieve our goal by copying the contents of Collection into a new class, WidgetCollection

```
abstract class WidgetCollection extends Widget {
    forEach(f); // perform the function f on each element of the collection
    where(f) ...
    map(f) ....
}
```

but every time Collection was changed, we'd need to update WidgetCollection. In general, such copy/paste coding can lead to all sorts of problems—maintenance, type checking, legal issues etc. Happily, we can use mixins to address this issue.

Each Dart class has a mixin. The mixin, as noted, is the class-specific functionality defined in the class body. So we can graphically depict each class C with superclass S as

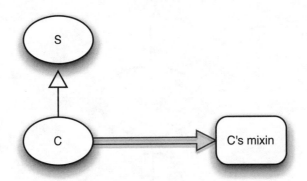

One way to look at a mixin is as a function that takes a superclass S and creates a new subclass of S with a particular body:

```
mixinCollection(S) { // ILLEGAL: just an illustration
  return class Collection extends S {
    forEach(f); // perform the function f on each element of the collection
    where(f) ...
    map(f) ....
}}
```

Each application of such a function to a given class yields a new subclass. We therefore speak of *mixin application* as the operation of deriving a class using a mixin and a superclass. We write S **with** M to denote the application of mixin M to superclass S. Obviously, S must name a class, but how do we name a mixin? By naming a class; the class implicitly defines a mixin via its body, and that is the mixin we'll apply to S.

We now know how to define CompoundWidget without replicating code.

```
class CompoundWidget extends Widget with Collection {
  ... compound widget stuff
}
```

The superclass of CompoundWidget is Widget **with** Collection, which is the mixin of class Collection applied to the superclass Widget, yielding a new, anonymous, class. The desired hierarchy now looks like

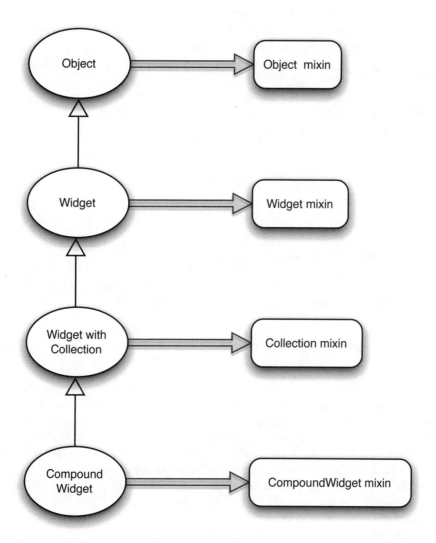

At the time of this writing, a class used as a mixin must not have an explicitly declared constructor. Violating this restriction will cause a compilation error. This restriction may be relaxed in the future.

2.15.1 Example: The Expression Problem

In this section we'll consider a classic design challenge known as *the expression problem* and see how mixins facilitate an elegant solution. The expression problem is so-named because the concrete example used is the implementation of a language of expressions. However, the issues the expression problem brings up are characteristic of a much broader set of programming examples.

Consider the following language of expressions:
$Expression \rightarrow Expression + Expression | Expression - Expression | Number$
An AST for this language might have the form

```
class Expression {}
```

```
class Addition extends Expression {
  var operand1, operand2;
}
```

```
class Subtraction extends Expression {
  var operand1, operand2;
}
```

```
class Number extends Expression { int val;}
```

Now suppose you want to define an evaluator for this language. You can define it in classic OO style by adding eval methods to each leaf class above:

```
get eval => operand1.eval + operand2.eval;  // in Addition
get eval => operand1.eval - operand2.eval; // in Subtraction
get eval => val; // in Number
```

This is problematic however. When you want to convert such expressions to strings, you need to add another method to the original hierarchy. There is an unbounded number of similar functions and your classes will rapidly become unwieldy. Besides, not everyone who wants to define new functionality has access to the original source code.

An alternative is to define the evaluator as a function outside of the AST classes. You would have to test the incoming expression to see what type it was, then take the appropriate action. This is tedious and inefficient, and so one typically uses the visitor pattern instead. Regardless, this organization has a dual problem: although adding functions is easy, adding new types is hard.

The dilemma is illustrated in the following table:

Class\Function	eval	toString()
Addition	operand1.eval + operand2.eval	'$operand1 + $operand2'
Subtraction	operand1.eval - operand2.eval	'$operand1 - $operand2'
Number	val	'$val'
Multiplication	operand1.eval * operand2	'$operand1 * $operand2'

Types correspond to rows in the table, and functions correspond to columns. The object-oriented style makes it easy to add rows, but adding columns is invasive. The functional style does the opposite—adding columns is easy, but adding rows is invasive.

What we really need is a way to add individual entries to the table independently. The problem can be nicely addressed with mixins. The following Dart code shows how.

We start out with three initial datatypes, but we define them as abstract classes because these won't be the datatypes we actually instantiate. They serve to define the structure of the types and their constructors.

```
library abstract_expressions;


abstract class AbstractExpression{};
abstract class AbstractAddition {
  var operand1, operand2;
  AbstractAddition(this.operand1, this.operand2);
}


abstract class AbstractSubtraction {
  var operand1, operand2;
  AbstractSubtraction(this.operand1, this.operand2);
}


abstract class AbstractNumber {
  var val;
  AbstractNumber(this.val);
}
```

Now let's define our first function, the evaluator. We'll do this via a set of mixin classes.

```
library evaluator;


abstract class ExpressionWithEval {
  get eval;
 }


abstract class AdditionWithEval  {
  get operand1;
  get operand2;
  get eval => operand1.eval + operand2.eval;
}


abstract class SubtractionWithEval  {
  get operand1;
  get operand2;
  get eval => operand1.eval - operand2.eval;
}
```

```
abstract class NumberWithEval {
  get val;
  get eval => val;
}
```

The evaluator above is completely independent of the type hierarchy; notice we have not imported so much as a single dependency.

The actual types our clients should use are defined separately

```
library expressions;
```

```
import 'abstractExpressions.dart';
import 'evaluator.dart';
```

```
abstract class Expression = AbstractExpression with ExpressionWithEval;
```

```
class Addition = AbstractAddition with AdditionWithEval implements Expression;
```

```
class Subtraction = AbstractSubtraction with SubtractionWithEval
                                      implements Expression;
```

```
class Number = AbstractNumber with NumberWithEval implements Expression;
```

Each concrete AST type is defined as a mixin application, extending the appropriate abstract datatype with the corresponding evaluator mixin.

We can add a main() function to expressions that builds a simple expression tree. This is possible because the various AST node classes have synthetic constructors implicitly defined for them based on the constructors of their superclasses.

```
main(){
  var e = new Addition(new Addition(new Number(4), new Number(2)),
                       new Subtraction(new Number(10), new Number(7))
             );
}
```

What is the point of the separation of abstract and concrete types? The role of expressions is to define our overall system by connecting its various components via mixin application. The role of abstractExpressions is to define the form of our AST nodes. Keeping these separate will allow us to extend the system by modifying expressions without touching our datatype representation.

The general pattern is that each concrete class is based on extending an abstract class that defines its data representation, with a series of mixins representing all the functions on that datatype. The approach works because we define a separate mixin for each combination of function and type. For example, above, each eval method is defined in its own mixin class.

If we want to add a type, we can do so independently. We will add an AST node for multiplication:

```
library multiplication;


abstract class AbstractMultiplication {
  var operand1, operand2;
  AbstractMultiplication(this.operand1, this.operand2);
}
```

Again the addition is completely independent of the original class hierarchy and of any functions. At this stage, we also have to define how multiplication is evaluated. We can define that as a separate library

```
library multiplication_evaluator;


abstract class MultiplicationWithEval {
  get operand1;
  get  operand2;
  get eval => operand1.eval * operand2.eval;
}
```

which again, is completely independent. We do need to create the corresponding concrete class in expressions.

```
class Multiplication = AbstractMultiplication with MultiplicationWithEval
                               implements Expression;
```

As you can see, it follows the same pattern as all the other types. We will need to add the following imports to expressions for the above to be valid.

```
import 'multiplication.dart';
import 'multiplicationEvaluator.dart';
```

The rest of the expressions library remains unchanged.

It would be nice to print the tree we build in main(). We can modify main() to do this; we'll also change our code to make use of the new type.

```
main(){
  var e = new Multiplication(new Addition(new Number(4), new Number(2)),
                      new Subtraction(new Number(10), new Number(7))
            );
  print('$e = ${e.eval}');
}
```

The print-out is less informative than we would like, since *e* is printed out using the default implementation of toString() inherited from Object. To address this, we can add a specialized implementation of toString() to our class hierarchy.

```
library string_converter;

abstract class ExpressionWithStringConversion {
  toString();
}

abstract class AdditionWithStringConversion {
  get operand1;
  get operand2;
  toString() => '($operand1 + $operand2)';
}


abstract class SubtractionWithStringConversion {
  get operand1;
  get operand2;
  toString() => '($operand1 - $operand2)';
}


abstract class NumberWithStringConversion {
  get val;
  toString() => '$val';
}


abstract class MultiplicationWithStringConversion {
  get operand1;
  get operand2;
  toString() => '($operand1 * $operand2)';
}
```

Again, we follow the formula of defining a mixin per method/type combination. This time, we know that the hierarchy involves multiplication and have defined the corresponding case in the same library as the other cases. Likewise, we'll want to refine expressions to integrate the new functionality.

```
library expressions;

import 'abstractExpressions.dart';
import 'evaluator.dart';
import 'multiplication.dart';
import 'multiplicationEvaluator.dart';
import 'stringConverter.dart';
```

abstract class Expression = AbstractExpression **with**
              ExpressionWithEval, ExpressionWithStringConversion;

class Addition = AbstractAddition **with**
    AdditionWithEval, AdditionWithStringConversion **implements** Expression;

class Subtraction = AbstractSubtraction **with**
    SubtractionWithEval, SubtractionWithStringConversion **implements** Expression;

class Number =   AbstractNumber **with**
           NumberWithEval, NumberWithStringConversion **implements** Expression;

class Multiplication =
   AbstractMultiplication **with** MultiplicationWithEval,
              MultiplicationWithStringConversion **implements** Expression;

Our main function remains unchanged, but it now prints a nice description of the tree:

((4 + 2) * (10 - 7)) = 18

One can continue the process of extension as desired. You can add as many types as you want, and as many functions as you want. You just have to define the final forms of the types you are going to use as mixin applications as shown above. For each type, the corresponding case for every function is defined by a separate mixin class. Adding a new function does require modifying those mixin applications, but this is really more like tweaking your make files to include the additional functions and/or types. If new types and new functions are defined independently, we can always define a mixin that adds the logic for applying the new function to the new type separately and mix it in as well.

In terms of the table, each mixin represents an individual entry, and each mixin application composes a row of the table.

We will revisit this design again when we discuss types in Chapter 5.

2.16   Related Work

As noted in the introduction, Dart's object model is heavily influenced by that of Smalltalk[1]. Smalltalk was the first pure object-oriented language, and many of the ideas here are directly tied to it. The notion of a metaclass hierarchy that circles back on itself originates there though Dart's metaclass hierarchy is rather simple compared to Smalltalk's. Unlike Smalltalk, instance construction is handled via constructors rather than methods, following the tradition established by C++. However, we address the major flaw of classic constructors, their inability to produce objects that are not freshly allocated by their class.

The use of noSuchMethod() is closely modeled after Smalltalk's doesNotUnderstand:. The notion of representation independence can be traced back to the language Self.

However, Dart does not uphold the principle of uniform reference, due to the influence of Javascript and the C style syntax.

Mixins originated as an idiom in certain Lisp dialects. The linguistic model of mixins used here was introduced by William Cook and the author in 1990[4], and first implemented in Strongtalk[5],[6], an innovative Smalltalk system with a particularly strong influence on Dart. Closely related constructs exist in languages such as Newspeak, Scala (where they are called traits) and Ruby.

The name "expression problem" is due to Philip Wadler. The expression problem has been discussed extensively in the literature ([7], [8], [9]). Proposed solutions vary depending on the language and requirements involved.

2.17 Summary

Dart is a pure object-oriented, class-based language, which means that all runtime values are objects and every object is an instance of some class.

Objects have state and behavior. The state is only available via special accessor methods—getters and setters. This ensures that all computation on Dart objects is done via a procedural interface.

Classes are reified at runtime and so must be objects themselves. Hence every class is an instance of a metaclass of type **Type**. Every class has at least one constructor; constructors are used to create objects. Some objects are constant, meaning they can be pre-computed at compile-time.

Every Dart class has a unique superclass, except for the root of the class hierarchy, **Object**. All Dart objects inherit common behavior from **Object**.

Dart supports mixin-based inheritance: every class induces a mixin capturing its unique contribution to the class hierarchy. Mixins allow the code of a class to be reused in a modular fashion independent of its place in the class hierarchy.

Chapter 3
Libraries

Dart programs are organized into modular units called *libraries*. We saw our first library in Chapter 1. You might imagine this was the **points** library shown at the end of that chapter, but in fact, it was our "Hello World" program. A trivial library perhaps, but a library all the same. Here it is again:

```
main(){
  print('Hello World');
}
```

As you can see, there is no requirement for an explicit library declaration like the one we saw in **points**. Most libraries do have such a declaration, which is useful for various reasons we shall illustrate below. However, for quick, simple tasks, it is convenient to be able to just write a function and run it. In Dart we always seek to enable experimentation with the language with a minimum of fuss, while still providing support for good software engineering practice.

3.1   The Top Level

In our example, the library consists of a single top-level function **main()**. In general, a library consists of a number of *top-level declarations*. These declarations may define functions, variables and types.

Here is a slightly larger, but still trivial example—a library that implements a stack. It's the kind of dreary exercise you might see in an introductory programming class, which is good, because we can focus on the language constructs rather than on sophisticated program logic.

```
library stack1;
final _contents = [];
get isEmpty => _contents.isEmpty;
get top => isEmpty ? throw 'Cannot get top of empty stack' : _contents.last;
get pop => isEmpty? throw 'Cannot pop empty stack' : _contents.removeLast();
push(e) {
  _contents.add(e);
  return e;
}
```

We have one top-level variable, _contents, which is initialized to an empty list. Top-level variables induce implicit accessors, much as instance and class fields do. Again, no user code accesses the variables directly. Top-level variables are initialized lazily, the first time their getter is called, just like class variables. In stack1, _contents won't be set to [] until one of the methods that access it is called.

Together, top-level and class variables constitute the category of static variables. The two differ in their scope—where they may be referenced by name. Whereas the names of class variables are restricted to the scope of the class that declared them (not even subclasses see them), the names of top-level variables (also known as *library variables*) are in scope throughout the library that declares them. The library scope typically comprises multiple classes and functions.

As with class variables, top-level variables may be final, in which case no setter is defined for them and they must be initialized at their point of declaration. It is also possible to declare a static variable (be it a class or library variable) as a constant, in which case it can only be assigned a compile-time constant and is treated as a constant (Sections 2.11, 6.1.4).

The scope rules for top-level functions (often referred to as *library methods*) are the same as for top-level variables; a top-level function is in scope throughout the library. One can define regular functions, getters and setters. In each case, the body of the function can be given in the short form using => followed by a single expression (as in isEmpty, top, pop), or by a sequence of statements between curly braces (as in push()).

In addition to top-level functions and variables, we also have top-level class declarations. All class declarations in Dart are top-level since Dart does not support nested classes.

3.2   Scripts

The "Hello World" program is an example of a *script*, which is a directly executable Dart library. A script begins executing at its main() function. If a library doesn't have a main() function, it is, by definition, not a script and it cannot be run on its own.

Scripts have one further peculiarity. The first line of a script may start with the character # that can be followed by arbitrary text up to the end of the line. This is useful in many environments which are able to run various interpreters on files, based on a # prefixed directive at the head of the file to be interpreted.

3.3   Privacy

Libraries are Dart's unit of encapsulation. Names that begin with an underscore (_) are private to a library. We saw an example above, the library variable _contents. Making _contents private helps maintain the integrity of the stack abstraction introduced by stack1. Because only the code inside stack1 can access _contents, we are assured that no other code will tamper with the underlying representation of the stack.

As another example, consider

```
class CachingClass {
  var _cache;
  operator [](i) {
    if (_cache[i] == null) {_cache[i]= complicatedFunction(i);}
    return _cache[i];
  }
}
```

No one outside the library that defines CachingClass can get at the _cache field.

This scheme allows you (and the compiler or any other tool) to recognize whether something is private without having to look up its declaration.

Privacy should not be confused with security. The purpose of privacy in Dart is to support software engineering needs, not security needs. The only security boundaries are those between isolates, which we will examine in detail in Chapter 8. Within an isolate, there are no security guarantees.

3.4 Imports

Readers are no doubt familiar with the concept of imports in programming. For example, if we wanted to make use of stack1 in an application, we might write

```
import 'stack1.dart';
main() {
  push('gently');
  push('harder');
  print(pop);
  print(top);
}
```

providing our main() function with access to the push() and pop methods of stack1. The script will print harder and then print gently. This code will work provided that the library stack1 is stored in a file named stack1.dart in the same directory as our main script. However, what if stack1 was stored elsewhere, say somewhere on the web such http://staxRUs/stack1.dart?

We could replace the import with:

```
import 'http://staxRUs/stack1.dart';
```

Dart imports work with arbitrary URIs (Universal Resource Indicators). However, neither of the URIs above is particularly advisable because it makes your code sensitive to any change in the imported library's location. Using such URIs is useful for quick and dirty experiments, but serious code requires more discipline. Typically, one would write

```
import 'package:stack1.dart';
```

The schema **package:** is used to invoke a resident *package manager* that encapsulates the knowledge of where code resides. Dart environments typically come with a package manager, but the details are outside the scope of this book.

There is no need to use the **package:** schema for libraries that are part of the Dart platform. These are accessed using the **dart:** schema, as in:

```
import 'dart:io';
```

Other examples include **dart:html, dart:json** and a good many others.

Whatever schema you use, the URI had better refer to an actual library, or a compiler error will occur. The URI also needs to be a constant string literal (6.1.1.4), and may not involve interpolation.

The names available within a library are those names it declares and those names introduced into the library scope via imports of other libraries. The names defined by **dart:core** are imported implicitly.

The set of names a library makes available to its clients differs from the names available internally. First, the names a library imports are not transitively made available to clients that import the library. Also, private members of a library are not available to other libraries that import them. There are additional differences we shall see shortly. It is therefore useful to speak of the *exported namespace* of a library.

Suppose we had an alternate stack implementation in a library **stack2**. We might write some code designed to test the two implementations. We might start by sketching out our script like this:

```
import 'package:stack1.dart';
import 'package:stack2.dart';
main() {}
```

So far, so good. You can compile this code without any issues. However, once we try to fill out the body of **main()** with code that uses the imports, we will hit a snag.

```
import 'package:stack1.dart';
import 'package:stack2.dart';
main() {
  // testing stack1
  push('gently'); // Static warning
  push('harder'); // Static warning
  print(pop); // Static warning
  print(top);  // Static warning
  // testing stack2
  push('gently'); // Static warning
  push('harder'); // Static warning
  print(pop); // Static warning
  print(top); // Static warning
}
```

Can you tell the difference between the code that uses stack1 and the code that uses stack2? Of course not, and neither can the compiler. The methods of stack2 have the same names as those of stack1, and importing them both into the same scope is hopelessly ambiguous.

The Dart compiler will issue a warning about every use of the ambiguous names. Notice that importing conflicting names does not in itself cause any warning—warnings are issued only if you try to use an ambiguous name. This is in keeping with Dart's "keep out of the way" philosophy. It also has the nice property that when someone adds a top-level name to a library you imported earlier, your code is less likely to break.

If we ignore the warnings and try to run the code, the first call to push() will result in a runtime error. Specifically, a NoSuchMethodError will be raised, because push() is not well defined. Readers might well ask why is the code even allowed to run? We know with certainty that it will fail, so why not mark these situations as errors and refuse to compile the program?

Bear in mind that the use of an ambiguous name might be in a branch that is not always executed. Should we prevent a developer from testing another branch until the ambiguity is eliminated? We think not; we do not want to impose a specific workflow on the programmer. Instead, we are content to inform programmers of the problem, and leave it to them to decide when to resolve it. In general, Dart seeks to avoid compilation errors as much as it can in order to avoid imposing a specific ordering of tasks on the programmer.

A good way to overcome the kind of ambiguity shown above is to distinguish the two imports by providing each set of imported names with a distinct prefix.

```
import 'package:stack1.dart' as stack1;
import 'package:stack2.dart' as stack2;
main() {
  // testing stack1
  stack1.push('gently');
  stack1.push('harder');
  print(stack1.pop);
  print(stack1.top);
  // testing stack2
  stack2.push('gently');
  stack2.push('harder');
  print(stack2.pop);
  print(stack2.top);
}
```

Dart gives priority to the declarations within a library over any imports, so adding a top-level name to an imported library is not as damaging as it might be. Problems can still arise, however. Additions to an imported library can cause problems in your code if you access a name from one import, and another imported library later adds the same name. In addition, a newly imported name can shadow an inherited name.

Prefixing all imports ensures that when imported libraries add top-level members, they can never cause breakage to the importer in the future.

Prefixes may not conflict with any other top-level declaration in the enclosing library. The compiler will flag such conflicts as errors. Because local names have precedence over any imports, a prefix will shadow any declaration of the same name that is imported without a prefix.

It is permissible to use the same prefix on several imports. If the prefixed names introduced by these imports conflict, the same rules given above apply: no issues unless the conflicting names are used, in which case a warning is issued at compile time, and execution will fail with NoSuchMethod at runtime.

It is important to understand that Dart considers names to be in conflict only if they refer to distinct declarations. If we imported push() twice from the same library, no problem would arise either at compile-time or runtime.

Dart provides additional mechanisms to control what names are imported into a library: the *namespace combinators* **show** and **hide**. A *namespace* is a mapping from names to declarations. As an example, consider the namespace declared by stack1. This includes _contents, isEmpty, top, pop and push. When we import stack1, we don't see _contents because it is private; it is not part of the exported name space of stack1. Usually, an import provides the importer with access to the exported namespace of the imported library. Both prefixing and the namespace combinators allow us to manipulate the namespace being imported.

The **hide** combinator takes a namespace and a list of identifiers, producing a new namespace from which the listed identifiers have been dropped. If we were to include the following import in a library:

```
library lib1;
import 'stack1.dart' hide isEmpty, top;
```

only pop and push would be available in lib1 because the namespace being imported is no longer the complete exported namespace of stack1. The **hide** operator is applied to the exported namespace, eliminating isEmpty and top. It is the result of the application of **hide** that is in fact provided in the scope of the importer.

The **show** combinator is similar, except that only the listed identifiers are retained in the resulting namespace. We can use **show** to gain the same effect as the previous example:

```
library lib1;
import 'stack1.dart' show  pop, push;
```

In contrast, let's take

```
library lib1;
import 'stack1.dart' show isEmpty, top;
```

Here, only isEmpty and top are provided in lib1, whereas pop and push are not. This example could alternatively be expressed as:

```
library lib1;
import 'stack1.dart' hide  pop, push;
```

When should one use **show** and when **hide**? If you are importing a large library from which you only intend to use a handful of members, you may find **show** more convenient. In contrast, if you are trying to resolve a conflict or two between libraries, you may choose to use **hide**, but you're probably better off using **as** with a prefix to ensure conflicts never arise. However, as we'll see when we discuss exports below, **hide** has additional uses.

If you really want to make your library robust, you should combine prefixes with **show**, only importing elements you actually use

```
library lib1;
import 'stack1.dart' as stack1 show pop, push;
```

This way, you can tell exactly what members you are dependent upon by glancing at the top of your library. Most programmers may find this level of discipline a tad tedious, but good development tools should be able to maintain such imports for you automatically.

One may find accessing imports via prefixes too verbose. An alternate style insists on always using **show**, but without prefixes. Use of **show** will prevent any new members of an import from causing inadvertent conflicts. However, one may still have to resolve conflicts between members from different imports, and beware of conflicts between imports and inherited members.

3.5   Breaking Libraries into Parts

Sometimes a library is just too large to conveniently keep in a single file. Dart lets you break libraries into smaller components called *parts*. Suppose we have a Dart library implementing an interactive development environment (IDE) for Dart. The IDE includes class browsers, object inspectors, a debugger, as well as integrated support for unit testing, package management and version control. This is a large program, and we definitely don't want one monstrous file holding it all. At the same time, due to the tight integration, we might want the IDE to be a single library, with its own private state shared across its subsystems. We could structure it as follows:

```
library ide;
import 'dart:io' as io;
import 'dart:mirrors' as mirrors;
import 'dart:async' as async;
// many more: UI etc.
part 'browsing.dart';
part 'inspecting.dart';
part 'debugging.dart';
part 'unitTestIntegration.dart';
part 'packages.dart';
part 'vcs.dart';
```

Each subsystem resides in its own file, and the library is defined by referencing all of them using the **part** directive. Each **part** directive gives a URI where the part may be found. The URIs follow the same rules as those in imports. Parts share the same scope—the internal namespace of the library that referenced them, including any imports.

It might seem as if the **part** is similar to the #include directives of C. This is not the case however. Parts are structured. Each part must begin with a *part header* that specifies what library the part belongs to. For example, 'browsing.dart' might start out with

```
part  of ide;
 // top-level declarations
 class ClassBrowser ...

  ...
```

The part header refers to its library using the library's name. Not all libraries have a name, but if one wants a library built out of parts, it must be given a name. Parts should be well structured, logical groupings, not arbitrary blobs of code.

What if the part is referenced from a different library? For instance, suppose packages.dart reads:

```
// file packages.dart
part  of packageManager;
 // top-level declarations
 class Package ...

  ...
```

This sort of mistake can certainly happen, and will give rise to a warning from the Dart compiler. As usual, Dart tries to avoid full-blown compilation errors that preclude execution. It may be that you've found a part like packages.dart useful in a context other than its original library. In the long term, this is probably a bad idea, since updates to packages.dart might conflict with your plans for the ide library. However, it might be very handy as a temporary measure to get things going. It can certainly be compiled and run, and Dart is not going to stand in your way.

Another problem that could arise is that packages.dart was in fact not a part at all:

```
// file packages.dart
library packages;
 // top-level declarations
 class Package ...

  ...
```

This code will lead to a compile-time error, because there is nothing sensible the compiler can do in this situation. The general rule is that it is a compilation error if a library refers to a part at some URI, and the contents of that URI are not a part, and it is warning if the part does not refer back to the same library. As with imports (and exports, as we'll see next) it is also a compile-time error if the URI is not a constant string or involves string interpolation.

3.6   Exports

Let's consider our IDE example again. IDEs need not be massive multimillion line-of-code edifices, but they can be. It is possible that our project may grow beyond our wildest expectations, and we really need to split it into multiple libraries. It is also possible that we want to provide third parties an API to the IDE.

Of course, one can import the various component libraries of the IDE as needed. However, these APIs may be large and complex, and we might want to provide a more manageable subset. This is also useful when we don't want to burden our users with importing a slew of sublibraries. Also, we may not want to expose the internal library structure of our project.

How do we compose a manageable API out of a series of libraries?

```
library ideAPI;

export 'browsing.dart'
   show  AbstractBrowser, LibraryBrowser, ClassBrowser;
export 'inspecting.dart' show  ObjectInspector;
export 'debugging.dart' show  ThreadBrowser, ActivationBrowser;
export 'unitTestIntegration.dart' show  TestBrowser, TestSuite;
export 'packages.dart' show  PackageBrowser;
export 'vcs.dart' show  RepositoryBrowser;
```

The **export** directive allows a library to augment its exported namespace with additional names from other namespaces. In cases like ideAPI, the entire purpose of a library is to aggregate and package features of other libraries in a conveniently consumable form. It does so by building up an API out of the exported namespaces of several libraries, suitably filtered using **show** and **hide**. While our example only uses **show**, in a scenario where we were exporting a large API but wanted to avoid a conflict with another exported library, **hide** would be very useful.

However, using **hide** has a disadvantage: if a new member were added to the exported library, it could give rise to conflicts. On the other hand, the advantage of **hide** is that we do not explicitly have to update our export clauses to make additions to the exported library available to our clients.

Notice that ideAPI doesn't import anything. Exports are completely independent of imports. You can export a library even if you make no use of it in your library. That is exactly what enables libraries like ideAPI to aggregate (parts of) multiple APIs.

The rules for exports echo those for imports and parts: the URI used in an export must refer to a library and must be a constant string literal that does not involve interpolation. The compiler will report an error if any of these requirements are violated. It is also a compilation error if a library exports a name via several export clauses. This situation is inherently ambiguous—what entity will we actually be exporting?

3.7   Diamond Imports

When importing several such aggregate APIs, one might end up importing the same entity via several pathways. This situation is known as *diamond import* and is illustrated below.

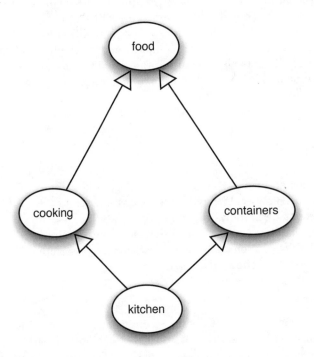

```
library food;

class Escargot {...}
class Caviar {...}
class Pasta  {...}
class IceCream {...}
class IceCreamCone {
   fill(contents){ ...}
}


library cooking;
import 'package:food.dart' as food
    show Escargot, Caviar, Pasta, IceCream, IceCreamCone;
export 'package:food.dart'
    show Escargot, Caviar, Pasta, IceCream, IceCreamCone;
```

```
class CoqAuVin {...}
class SeaBassInBaroloSauce {...}
class PeaSoup {...}
class RabbitBrainsWithAnemone {...}
class SpaghettiBolognese {...}


library containers;
export 'package:food.dart' show IceCreamCone;

class Plate {...}
class Cup {...}
class Bowl {...}

library kitchen;
import 'package:containers.dart';
import 'package:food.dart';

makeIceCream() {
  new IceCreamCone().fill(new IceCream());
}
```

The kitchen library imports both cooking and containers. Each includes the name IceCreamCone in its exported namespace. Dart will warn about this situation; however, it is not considered an error because both got IceCreamCone from food and simply re-exported it.

Consider what happens if containers decides to replace the version of IceCreamCone from food with another (say by declaring its own version, or obtaining IceCreamCone from another provider). The containers library has maintained its public API unchanged, and so clients should not experience any difficulties. However, the change would suddenly render the code above illegal.

This is undesirable, and for this reason we issue a warning. However, in typical Dart style, we do not preclude compilation, since there is no real ambiguity. The warning is useful so that the programmer does not overlook the potential conflict. It encourages best practice, which is to avoid ambiguity at all times.

3.8 Deferred Loading

Sometimes it is necessary to defer the loading of a library. The reasons vary. Often, we simply want to keep the initial download as small as possible in the interest of fast application startup. Another situation can arise in large applications with a lot of functionality; it may be that certain features are not utilized by all users, and so the library that implements that feature is not always required. Not loading a library that is not used helps reduce memory usage.

Dart supports these scenarios using *deferred imports*.

import 'rarelyUsed.dart' **deferred as** rarelyUsed;

The import is still used by the compiler during development to bring the required names into scope, but attempting to access these names at runtime will cause a dynamic error unless they are explicitly loaded.

A deferred import must always provide a prefix. The prefix provided may not be used by any other import in the library. Violating these rules causes a compile-time error.

When the time comes to actually use the deferred library (say, when the user chooses a menu entry that requires that functionality), we can invoke the loadLibrary() method on rarelyUsed.

rarelyUsed.loadLibrary().then(onLoad);

where onLoad is defined as

onLoad(loadSucceeded) => loadSucceeded ? doStuff() : makeExcuses();

The call to loadLibrary() is asynchronous. It initiates loading of the library, but returns immediately rather than waiting until loading has completed. The result of loadLibrary() is a *future*—an object that is a placeholder for a value that will be available at a later time. Futures will be described in detail in Chapter 8. For now, what we need to know is that futures support a method then() which takes a function valued argument. When the value the future represents is finally available, that function will be called with the actual value.

In our case, the future returned by loadLibrary() is a placeholder for a Boolean that indicates whether loading succeeded. After the loading process completes (successfully or unsuccessfully), the function onLoad() will be called. Its parameter, loadSucceeded, will be bound to the aforementioned Boolean value, telling us whether the library is in fact loaded or not. We then choose our course of action appropriately. For example, doStuff() might be written as:

doStuff(){ rarelyUsed.respondToMenuRequest();}

It is crucial that we avoid accessing rarelyUsed unless we know it has been loaded. If we try to access it before loading completes, we will get a runtime error. We might choose to reference rarelyUsed only within doStuff(), thereby reducing the risk of premature access. We still run the risk that doStuff() might be called elsewhere, before rarelyUsed has been loaded.

3.9 Related Work

Dart's imports are conventional, except for their reliance on URIs instead of built-in identifiers as in most older languages. The traditional strengths and weaknesses of imports carry over to Dart. For example, it is not possible to have multiple copies of the same library tied to different dependencies within the same address space. Dart's support for isolates may alleviate this problem somewhat. On the other hand, imports are concrete and recognized by most programmers.

Diamond import is related to, yet different from, the diamond inheritance problem ([10], [11]).

Dart's approach to privacy is original. It deviates from the long tradition of class based privacy as found in C++, Java and C#. It also differs from the Smalltalk model of object-based privacy, and from privacy models based upon abstract datatypes (ADTs) such as those used in CLU, Ada, Modula and Oberon among many others.

The approach is pragmatic. It deals well with interactions among multiple classes without relying on a type system. In the absence of a mandatory static type system, class-based encapsulation requires expensive dynamic checks, so dynamically typed object-oriented languages tend toward either object-based encapsulation, or making everything public. The former option was deemed to be too austere a discipline, while the latter is unsuited to a language designed for serious software engineering.

The namespace combinators **show** and **hide** follow in a long tradition. Examples include the module combinators in [12], the operations on traits[13], the operations on units in Racket[14], and no doubt others.

3.10 Summary

Dart programs consist of libraries. A library aggregates classes/types, functions and variables. Dart libraries are units of privacy rather than security.

Execution of a Dart program always begins with the main() function of its script. Libraries may be split into multiple parts. Dart libraries connect to their dependencies via imports, and can selectively import names from other libraries by invoking namespace combinators and using prefixes to distinguish among imports. Libraries can also re-export other libraries or subsets thereof, again utilizing namespace combinators. Loading of libraries may be deferred at runtime to improve startup time and/or reduce footprint.

Chapter 4

Functions

Functions are the workhorse of Dart. It is functions that actually compute things. We use the term *functions* loosely to cover functions and methods of all syntactic forms, regardless of whether they behave as mathematical functions or not.

Functions in Dart are first class values that can be stored in variables, passed as parameters and returned as results. Like all runtime values in Dart, functions are objects.

We have already encountered a variety of functions: top-level functions, instance and class methods (be they getters, setters, operators or vanilla methods) and constructors. As we shall see, there are also local functions and function literals. They all share common structure which we will illustrate here.

4.1 Parameters

A function always has a list of *formal parameters*, though the parameter list may be empty, and for getter methods it is elided. Parameters are either *positional* or *named*.

4.1.1 Positional Parameters

Parameters may be *required* or *optional*. Here are some functions with required parameters:

```
zero() => 0; // a function with no parameters; technically, it has 0 parameters
get zero => 0; // another version of the same thing
id(x) => x; // The identity function;
identity(x) {return x;} // a more verbose identity function
add(a, b) => a + b; // a function with two required parameters
```

Optional parameters must all be listed together at the end of the parameter list in between square brackets. Any required parameters must precede the optional ones. Optional parameters can be given default values, which must be compile time constants.

```
increment(x, [step = 1]) => x + step; // step is optional, defaults to 1
```

We can call increment() with either one or two arguments.

```
increment(1); // evaluates to 2
increment(2, 4); // evaluates to 6
increment(); // runtime error
increment(2, 3, 4); // runtime error
```

The first call binds x to 1; since the second argument was not provided, **step** gets bound to its default value of 1, yielding $1 + 1 = 2$. The second call obviously yields $2 + 4 = 6$. The third call raises a NoSuchMethodError when executed. Even though we have a function named increment in scope, we don't have one that takes zero arguments, and so an exception is thrown. The situation with respect to the final call is similar; there is no version of increment() that accepts three parameters.

4.1.2 Named Parameters

Parameters may be positional or named. We have already seen many examples of positional parameters. Named parameters are less common in programming languages, which is why we have held back on introducing them until now. Named parameters are declared after any positional parameters, between curly braces.

Here is an example that relies exclusively on named parameters:

```
addressLetter({name: '', street: '', number, city, zip, country}) {
  var addr = new Address();
  addr.street = street;
  addr.number = number;
  addr.city = city;
  addr.zip = zip;
  addr.country = country;
  return addr;
}
addressLetter(street: "Downing", number: 10);
addressLetter(street: "Wall", city: "New York", country: "USA");
addressLetter(city: "Paris", country: "France");
addressLetter(name: "Alice", country: "Wonderland");
addressLetter();
addressLetter(name: "room", number: 101, country: "Oceania");
```

As the code shows, one can invoke addressLetter() with any combination of named parameters—including all or none.

The following example shows a case where required and named parameters are mixed.

```
var map = new Map();
fail() => throw('Key not found');
lookup(key, {ifMissing: fail}) {
  var result = map[key];
  if (result == null) {return ifMissing();}
  return result;
}
```

Often, a callback function such as an error handler is specified via a named parameter, while the other formals are given positionally.

```
lookup("anything"); // throws
lookup("anything", ifMissing: () => map["anything"] = 42); // 42
```

If we wanted to give a better error message, we might want to write

```
var map = new Map();
lookup(key, {ifMissing}) {
  var result = map[key];
  if (result != null) {return result;}
  return ifMissing == null? throw '$key not found' : ifMissing();
}
```

In this variant, we take advantage of the fact that if no default value is specified for an optional parameter, it will default to **null**.

Named parameters are always optional. In other words, the classification of parameters as required vs. optional is not orthogonal to their classification as positional vs. named. You cannot mix optional positional parameters with named parameters—you either use one kind or the other.

Formal parameters are not **final**. They can be mutated just like any other variable; however this should be avoided as a matter of good style. One should seek to minimize the use of mutable variables; mutation makes code harder to understand and reason about.

4.2 Function Bodies

A function has a body containing code to be evaluated when the function is executed. The body follows the signature, and can come in the two forms we've seen:

1. A list of statements (possibly empty) enclosed in curly braces.

2. A single expression following the token =>.

In the first form, execution begins with the first statement in the body and continues until the first of the following things happens: either the last statement in the function has been successfully executed, a **return** statement is executed, or an exception that is not caught inside the function is thrown.

Every function in Dart either returns a value or throws an exception.

If we finish the last statement and it is not a **return**, we return **null** from the function. For example

```
sideEffect(){
  print("I don't have a return and I don't throw an exception");
```

```
    print( "What is my value?" );
  }
  sideEffect(); // prints and then evaluates to null
```

Constructors are special functions used to create instances of classes. Constructors include factories, which are normal functions accorded a special role, and generative constructors. Generative constructors differ in that they always return a fresh instance or throw an exception. So a generative constructor does not return **null** in the absence of an explicit **return** statement. Indeed, a generative constructor cannot return an arbitrary expression. It may only include a **return** statement if that statement has no associated expression.

4.3   Function Declarations

Most of the functions we've seen so far have been introduced by function declarations. The exceptions have been constructors, getters and setters. A function declaration has a name that is followed by a parameter list and a body.

Abstract methods consist of a function signature but provide no body. Abstract methods are not technically function declarations. They serve only as declarations that help guide the static analyzer.

Function declarations can occur at the top level (e.g., main()) or as methods, and we have encountered many examples. However, functions may also be *local functions*. Local functions are function definitions nested within other functions.

Here is a simple example—defining a nested auxiliary function when computing the Fibonacci sequence:

```
  fib(n) {
    lastTwo(n) {
      if (n < 1) { return [0, 1]; }
      else {
        var p = lastTwo(n-1);
        return [p[1], p[0]+p[1]];
      }
    }
    return lastTwo(n)[1];
  }
```

This isn't the best way to compute the nth Fibonacci number but it does avoid the waste of the naive recursive version. Since lastTwo() is just an implementation detail of fib(), it is best to nest lastTwo() inside fib() and avoid polluting the surrounding namespace with an extra function name.

4.4 Closures

Functions can be defined inline as part of an expression. These are known as *function literals* or, more loosely, as *closures*. Unlike function declarations, closures are not named. However, they do have a parameter list and a body just like any other function.

```
(x) => x; // yet another identity function
(x){return x;} // and another
(x, [step = 1]) => x + step; // a closure with an optional parameter
(a, b) => a + b; // a closure with two required parameters
```

Looking at these examples in isolation, it may not be immediately clear how useful closures are. They look exactly like function declarations without names. The real benefit comes from using them as part of a larger expression.

Consider the problem of summing the elements of a list. One can certainly write a **for** loop to do this, but that is a rather primitive approach. A knowledgeable Dart programmer would instead write

```
sum(nums) => nums.reduce( (a, b) => a + b);
```

The reduce() method is defined for lists and many other types in Dart. Anything that implements Iterable should have a working reduce() method. The method takes a binary function, which we shall call combiner, as its argument. When invoked, reduce iterates over its receiver. Processing starts by taking the first two elements and feeding them to combiner. In each subsequent iteration, the result of the last call to combiner is passed as the first argument to a new call to combiner, along with the next element of the receiver. If combiner() adds its arguments, the effect is to add the first two elements of the receiver, then add the result to the third element and so on, producing the sum.

We could of course write sum without closures

```
sum(nums) { // bad style
  plus(a,b) => a + b;
  nums.reduce(plus);
}
```

which is slightly more verbose and requires us to name the addition function. In the case of addition, the name is obvious, but having to declare and name a function becomes increasingly onerous in examples like

```
country.cities.where((city) => city.population > 1000000);
```

which presumably finds all the cities in country with a population of over a million people. This snippet uses the where() method, another method from Iterable that takes a function as an argument. In this case, the argument must be a unary predicate, and where() will return those elements for which the predicate holds true.

4.5   Invoking Methods and Functions

Functions can be invoked in the standard way, by following a function valued expression with a parenthesized argument list, for example, print('Hello, oh brave new world that has such people in it').

Some functions, known as getters, can be invoked without a parameter list:

```
true.runtimeType; // bool
```

As we discussed earlier, the uniform use of getters and setters provides us the valuable property of representation independence. One should note, however, that unlike several other languages that support representation independence, Dart does not fully adhere to the principle of *uniform reference*. In Dart, one does not refer to methods and fields via a uniform syntax. While getters and fields are treated indistinguishably, ensuring representation independence, getters and methods are accessed via different syntax. Consequently, Dart programmers need to be aware if a function is declared as a getter or a nullary method. A similar argument holds for setters.

4.5.1   Cascades

In addition to the normal use of the dot operator for member selection, Dart supports the double-dot operator for *method cascades*. Cascades are useful when we need to perform a series of operations on a given object.

A cascade is evaluated just like an ordinary method invocation, except that it does not evaluate to the value returned by the method invocation, but rather to the receiver of the method invocation.

```
"Hello".length.toString(); // evaluates to '5'
"Hello"..length.toString(); // evaluates to "Hello"
```

Therefore, instead of

```
var address = new Address.of("Freddy Krueger");
address.setStreet("Elm", "13a");
address.city = "Carthage";
address.state = "Eurasia";
address.zipCode(66666, extend: 66666);
address;
```

we can write a single expression

```
new Address.of("Freddy Krueger")
  ..setStreet("Elm", "13a")
  ..city = "Carthage"
  ..state = "Eurasia"
  ..zipCode(66666, extend: 66666);
```

Cascades do more than just save a few keystrokes. They enable the creation of fluent APIs without preplanning. In the absence of cascades, methods must be designed to always return the receiver so that they can be chained. With cascades, we achieve the same effect as chaining independently of the return values of the individual methods in the API.

It's important to format cascades carefully so that the code is readable. One should not abuse the cascade syntax by putting a series of cascades on a single line or by excessive nesting.

Cascades are useful when working with so-called builder APIs, where a descriptor is created in steps, but the object being described is created in one fell swoop at the end of the building process.

Another use for cascades arises when we want to invoke a method on an object and get the original target back, but the method returns some other result. If we write

```
var sortedColors = ['red', 'green', 'blue', 'orange', 'pink'].sublist(1, 3).sort();
```

we will find that sortedColors is null because sort() is void. We could rearrange the code

```
var colors = ['red', 'green', 'blue', 'orange', 'pink'].sublist(1, 3);
colors.sort();
```

but is much nicer to simply use a cascade

```
var sortedColors = ['red', 'green', 'blue', 'orange', 'pink'].sublist(1, 3)..sort();
```

4.5.2   Assignment

It may not be obvious, but assignments in Dart are often function invocations, because assignment to fields is a sugar for setter method invocation.

The precise meaning of an assignment such as $v = e$ depends on the declaration of v. If v is a local variable or a parameter, it is just an old fashioned assignment. Otherwise, the assignment is a sugar for invoking the setter named v=.

Whether an assignment is valid will depend on whether the setter v is defined, or whether the variable v is final. Final variables may not be reassigned and do not induce setters.

Compound assignments such as i += 2 are defined in terms of ordinary assignment. See Section 6.1.6 for more details.

4.5.3   Using Operators

Dart supports user-defined operators, such as the + operator we defined for Point. User defined operators in Dart are actually instance methods that use special names and have special syntax when used. Declarations of such methods must be prefixed with the built-in identifier **operator**.

Apart from syntax, all the rules that pertain to instance methods apply to operators. The set of permissible operators is: <, >, <=, >=, ==, -, +, /, ~/, *, %, |, ^, &, <<, >>, []=, [], ~.

In addition, there are a number of fixed operators that cannot be defined by the programmer. These are &&, || and the increment and decrement operators ++ and --(both prefix and postfix).

Assignment isn't considered an operator for these purposes, though the compound assignments do rely on operators for their semantics.

Identity isn't an operator in Dart either. Instead, Dart provides the predefined function identical().

The precedence rules for operators are fixed and follow established conventions. Likewise their arity. Most operators are binary. The notable exceptions are unary minus and []=. The latter is used for situations similar to assignment into arrays or maps (or any indexed collection), and requires two arguments: an index and a new value. The case of - is special, since we support both binary and unary minus operations.

4.6   The Function Class

Function is an abstract class that acts as a common superinterface for all functions. Function does not have any instance methods declared. It does however declare the class method apply(), which takes a function and an argument list, and invokes the named function with the arguments supplied.

The signature of apply() is

```
static apply(Function function,
    List positionalArguments,
    [Map<Symbol, dynamic> namedArguments]
    );
```

You'll note that the formal parameters of apply() carry type annotations. It requires a function to call and a list of positional arguments (which might be empty). Named arguments may be provided via a map from names to actual arguments, which could be objects of any type. The last argument is optional. Most functions don't take any named arguments, so it is convenient if they need not be provided.

The apply() method provides a mechanism for calling functions with a dynamically determined argument list. This way, we can deal with argument lists whose arity is unknown at compile time.

4.6.1   Emulating Functions

As mentioned before, it is a key tenet of object-oriented programming that it is the behavior of an object that matters, not its provenance. Ideally, any object should be able to emulate any other. For example, instances of Proxy are designed to emulate the behavior of arbitrary objects. Since functions are objects, we should be able to emulate their behavior as well. How could we emulate a function with Proxy? The most common and important behavior for a function is what it does when invoked, but invocation is a built-in operation. We'd like to be able to write

```
var p = new Proxy((x) => x*2);
p(1); // we want 2
```

Happily, the code above works as expected, though nothing we've discussed so far explains why.

It turns out that function application translates to an invocation of a special method named call(). All true functions implicitly support a call() method whose signature is the same as the one declared by the function, and whose effect is to execute the function. In the example, p(1) is really p.call(1). Of course, we cannot treat p.call(1) as p.call.call(1) otherwise we'd recurse forever.

Since Proxy has no method **call**, noSuchMethod() is invoked, forwarding the call to the target of the proxy, which, being a function, has its own call() method.

Any class that declares a call() method is considered to implicitly implement class Function.

Note that Function does not declare a call() method. The reason is that there is no specific signature it could declare: call() can have differing arity and may or may not have optional arguments (be they positional or named) with varying defaults. So there really is no common declaration of call() that could be listed in Function. Instead, the call() method is treated specially by the language.

4.7 Functions as Objects

Dart is a purely object-oriented language and so all runtime values in Dart are objects, functions included. Functions support the methods declared in Object, in addition to the call() method described in the previous section.

In most cases, functions inherit the methods of Object unchanged. Implementations have some freedom with respect to the implementation of toString() on functions. They typically produce a reasonable description of the function, which may include its signature.

Because the implementations of == and hashCode are usually inherited, two functions are usually considered equal only if they are identical. It is difficult to do otherwise, as a general notion of semantic equality among functions is undecidable.

How do we know that two functions are identical? Let us look at some examples.

```
computeIdentityFunction() {
  return (x) => x;
}
```

Can we assume that two distinct invocations of computeIdentityFunction() yield identical results? The answer is no. While this case it seems "obvious" that the function is the same, in fact, a distinct function object may be allocated each time a function expression is evaluated. Similarly, a local function declaration introduces a new object in each dynamic scope that contains it. As an example, consider the local function increment in the code below.

```
makeCounter() {
  var counter = 0;
  increment() => ++counter;
  return increment;
}
```

Each call to makeCounter() returns a different increment function. In this case, it is clear we don't want the same function object, since each is tied to a different counter variable.

A top-level or static function declaration can be named, and that name always denotes the same object.

However, in some cases we can do better. Dart treats closures derived via property extraction specially. If (and only if!) two expressions o_1 and o_2 evaluate to the same object (i.e., o_1 and o_2 are identical), then Dart will ensure that for a given identifier m, if $o_1.m$ is legal, then $o_1.m == o_2.m$.

As an example, consider typical UI code that registers listener functions with the DOM. We want to be able to deregister a function after we have registered it. If we registered a regular closure as a listener

```
myElement.onClick.listen((event) => listener(event));
```

we could not deregister it later via a call such as

```
myElement.removeEventListener('onClick', (event) => listener(event));
```

because the closure we pass to removeEventListener() is not the same as the one we registered. Even though they look the same, each is a distinct object, and there is no general way to determine if two distinct function objects are equal. We would have to store the listener so we could use it to deregister later. However, using property extraction

```
myElement.onClick.listen(myObject.listener);
```

deregistration works as expected

```
myElement.removeEventListener('onClick', myObject.listener);
```

The implementation of noSuchMethod() is inherited from Object, as is that of runtimeType. Various classes may be used to represent functions in a Dart runtime. All these classes will implement Function but one cannot reliably expect equality or identity to hold between the runtime types of different functions.

```
f(x) { return  (x) => x;}
```

```
g() {
  h() => 42;
  h.runtimeType is Function; // true
```

```
    h.runtimeType == (() => 42).runtimeType; // don't bank on this being true
    g.runtimeType == h.runtimeType; // or this
    (() => 42).runtimeType == (() => 42).runtimeType; // or even this!
}
```

```
main(){
  f.runtimeType is Function; // true
  f(3).runtimeType is Function; // true
  g.runtimeType is Function; // true
  f(2).runtimeType == f.runtimeType; // maybe true, maybe not
  f.runtimeType == g.runtimeType; // unlikely as arities differ, but no promises
}
```

As the code above shows, one cannot be sure if the runtime types of any two functions are the same. What one can rely upon is that they all implement Function. Of course, equal functions have equal runtime types.

```
f(x) { return  (x) => x;}
```

```
g() {
  h() => 42;
  h.runtimeType == h.runtimeType; // true
  var x = (() => 42);
  x.runtimeType == x.runtimeType; // true
}
```

```
main(){
  f.runtimeType == f.runtimeType; // true
  g.runtimeType == g.runtimeType; // true
}
```

4.8   Generator Functions

Dart supports *generators*, which are functions that are used to generate values in a collection. Generators may be *synchronous* or *asynchronous*. Synchronous generators provide a syntactic sugar for producing iterators (4.8.1), whereas asynchronous generators do the same for streams (8.3).

Here we will focus on synchronous generators. We will defer discussion of asynchronous generators (8.6.2) to Chapter 8 which deals with all things asynchronous.

4.8.1   Iterators and Iterables

Iterators are objects that allow one to iterate over a collection in sequence, and nothing else. Iterators are especially convenient if one wants to produce the contents of a collection lazily. Collections that support iteration via iterators are known as *iterables*. Iterables must have a getter iterator that returns an iterator.

The **for-in** (6.2.3.1) loop will operate on any iterable object.

The interfaces of iterators and iterables are codified by the classes Iterator and Iterable respectively.

Producing an iterator is rather formulaic. One needs to define an iterable collection class and in particular one must define its iterator getter that returns (obviously) an iterator. That will, in turn, require you to define an iterator class, with a moveNext() method. As an example, here is a particularly excruciating way to print the natural numbers up to 20:

```
class NaturalsIterable {
  var n;
  NaturalsIterable.to(this.n);
  get iterator => new NaturalIterator(n);
}

class NaturalIterator {
  var n;
  var current = -1;
  NaturalIterator(this.n);
  moveNext() {
    if (current < n) {
      current++;
      return true;
    }
    return false;
  }
}

naturalsTo(n) => new NaturalsIterable.to(n);

main() {
  for (var i in naturalsTo(20)) {print(i);}
}
```

In fact, a well-typed example would implement the full Iterable interface and would be a good deal longer.

4.8.2   Synchronous Generators

To reduce the boilerplate engendered by iterators, Dart supports synchronous generator functions. Using a synchronous generator saves us the trouble of defining the two classes necessary to implement even the most basic iterator. We can define a synchronous generator function by marking its body with the modifier **sync***:

```
naturalsTo(n) sync* {
  var k = 0;
  while (k < n) yield k++;
}
```

When called, the function immediately returns an Iterable i from which one can obtain an iterator j. The first time someone calls moveNext() on j, the function body begins execution. Upon entering the loop, the **yield** statement (6.2.9) is executed, causing k to be incremented, appending the prior value of k to i and suspending execution of naturalsTo(). The next time moveNext() is called, execution of naturalsTo() resumes just after the **yield** and the loop repeats.[1]

It is important to understand that the body of a generator function executes after the function has returned a result to its caller. It is natural to ask what role does a **return** statement (6.2.8) play inside a generator? The answer is that **return** simply terminates the generator.[2]

There is no question as to the disposition of any value being returned. One cannot have a **return** statement return a value in a generator; such a statement will be flagged as an error by the compiler. It would not make any sense to allow such a statement, given that a value has already been returned to the caller, and the caller has already completed processing and has disappeared from the call stack.

Even though it runs after the function has returned a result to the caller, the function body is associated with the result and interacts with it. In a synchronous generator, the result is always an iterable. The generator is always associated with both that iterable and an iterator derived from it.

Yield statements inside a synchronous generator append objects to its associated iterable, and then suspend the body as shown above. Execution and resumption of the body is always initiated by a call to moveNext() on the associated iterator. When **yield** suspends the body, moveNext() returns **true** to its caller. When the generator terminates, moveNext() returns **false**.

---

1. There are better ways to implement this particular example; when the elements of the sequence are computed based upon natural numbers, there is a convenient constructor, Iterable.generate() that takes an integer n and a function f, and produces an iterable representing the sequence $f(0) \ldots f(n-1)$:

naturalsTo(n) => **new** Iterable.generate(n, (x) => x);

The point of our example, however, is to show all the machinery necessary when defining iterators in the general case, and how **sync*** methods can simplify that machinery.

2. In some cases, **return** may not cause termination because a **finally** clause (6.2.4) my change the flow of control.

4.9   Related Work

Functions as first-class values have a vast and illustrious history in programming languages. It is far beyond the scope of this book to explore the space of functional languages, which use such function values as their fundamental building block.

The notion of treating functions as objects goes back to Smalltalk[1] whose blocks are precursors of Dart closures. Smalltalk blocks originally suffered various restrictions which have been removed in modern dialects.

A key difference between Dart functions and its ancestors in the Smalltalk language family is the behavior of **return** inside a closure. Smalltalk supports *non-local returns*, meaning that a **return** executed within a closure exits the surrounding method, returning to that method's caller. As a result, it is possible to define control constructs as library functions that take functions as parameters. This is not possible in Dart. The decision to avoid non-local returns in Dart was made regretfully due to implementation limitations on the underlying web platform. See 6.2.8 for further details.

Notably, Scala[15] also supports non-local returns.

4.10   Summary

Dart functions are objects like all other runtime values in Dart. Functions in Dart may be declared to accept positional or named parameters. Positional parameters may be required or optional. Named parameters are always optional.

Functions are always lexically scoped and close over their environment. However, Dart functions are not suited to the implementation of user-defined control constructs due to the semantics of **return**.

Dart supports functions both as methods within classes and as independent structures. Methods may be associated with an instance (instance methods) or a class (class methods). Independent functions may be declared at the library level (top-level functions), as local functions within other functions, or via literal expressions.

All built-in operators are also functions, and most of them are defined as instance methods that may be overridden by the programmer. User-defined classes can be defined to behave like built-in function types by implementing the special method **call**. All Dart functions are considered to be members of the type Function.

Chapter 5
Types

Up to this point, we have not discussed types in any detail. We have been able to delay the discussion until now because Dart is optionally typed. In this chapter, we shall describe Dart's types, filling in many gaps in the story we have presented so far. We begin by explaining optional typing, perhaps Dart's most unusual characteristic.

5.1 Optional Typing

As noted in the introduction, a language is optionally typed if, and only if:

- Types are syntactically optional.
- Types have no effect on runtime semantics.

The latter point is far more significant than the former. Those accustomed to traditional statically typed languages may find this disconcerting at first. The point is subtle but crucial. It is a cornerstone of the Dart design.

First, it is essential that Dart can be used as a dynamically typed language; any program that can be written in such a language should be expressible in Dart. We expect code to evolve, gaining type annotations over time. If type annotations were to change the behavior of a Dart program, it is very likely that working programs might cease to function as expected as type annotations were added to them. This would discourage the use of type annotations, since programmers would fear that working code would malfunction.

Moreover, Dart programs will often include parts that are typed and parts that are not. This implies that one cannot assume type safety, and one cannot assume that a type annotation is in fact true. In such a situation, allowing type annotations to assume semantic significance could be confusing and destabilizing.

As an example of a language feature whose runtime behavior depends on types, consider type-based method overloading. Overloading is a common feature of statically typed object-oriented languages. In such a language, one might write

```
class NotLegalDart {
  overloaded(List l)=> l.length;
  overloaded(num n) => n*2;
}
```

and expect calls to resolve based on the type of the argument

```
int x = 3;
new NotLegalDart().overloaded(x); // presumably 6
List l = [];
new NotLegalDart().overloaded(l); // presumably 0
```

Now, what are we to make of

```
var x = 3;
new NotLegalDart().overloaded(x); // ?
var l = [];
new NotLegalDart().overloaded(l); // ??
```

On what basis are we to chose an implementation of overloaded? Presumably, this would be an error, forcing the user to specify types contrary to the notion of optional typing.[1]

Imagine further that we added a "catch-all" variant of overloaded

```
class NotLegalDart {
  ... as before
  overloaded(x) => x;
}
```

In this case, our second set of calls would resolve to the catch-all version, but if we decided to annotate the variables with types, the behavior would change just because we decided to document code at the call site.

Type based overloading is a problematic feature even in the presence of full static typing. Because types do not effect the semantics of Dart, the language cannot support type-based overloading. Consequently, all the examples we have shown will always behave the same in production, even if we decorate them with type annotations.

As another example consider

```
class LazyFields{
  var _x;
  get x => _x == null? _x = complicatedFunction() :_x;
}
```

Here we have a fairly common scenario where an instance variable is lazily initialized. Now suppose we decide to specify the type of _x:

```
class LazyFields{
  int _x;
```

---

1. Some might argue that we should consider the dynamic type of the argument in choosing the method. Such a mechanism, known as *multi-methods* has its own issues that are beyond the scope of this discussion.

```
    get x  => _x == null? _x = complicatedFunction() :_x;
}
```

In many languages, the type of a variable influences its default value. It is typical to initialize an integer variable to 0. Unfortunately, the code will stop working in that case. Because of such issues, Dart adheres to the principle that type annotations have no semantic effect.

5.2   A Tour of Types

Dart variables may have types associated with them. Types may also be used to indicate the return types of methods. For example

```
int sum(int a, int b) => a + b;
void main(){ print(sum(3,4));} // prints 7
```

We can of course write code without types, as we have seen repeatedly in the preceding chapters. Here is very similar code, differing only in the absence of type annotations:

```
sum(a, b) => a + b;
main(){ print(sum(3,4));} // prints 7
```

These two variants behave exactly the same. The human reader benefits from the documentation provided by the type annotations, but the runtime doesn't care.

Development tools, such as interactive development environments (IDEs) can take advantage of type annotations in various ways: they can issue warnings about possible inconsistencies, they can help the programmer by showing menus of methods that are potentially applicable to expressions (name completion) or by supporting automated code refactoring based on type information etc.

The simple example above contains no errors, so it is easy to see that the behavior of the two variants is the same. Suppose we change things a little

```
var i;
var j = 0;
sum(a, b) => a + b;
main(){ print(sum(i, j));} // NoSuchMethodError
```

Since i is not initialized, its value is null. When we execute sum, we end up calling the + method on null. Since + is not defined by Null, which is the class of null, we get a NoSuchMethodError. In some languages, you might get a null pointer error, but we know that in Dart, null, like all values, is an object and so it does respond to methods such as == etc.

The typed version below behaves identically at runtime. As discussed above, the fact that i is marked as an int does not change the way it is initialized.

```
int i;
int j = 0;
int sum(int a, int b) => a + b;
main(){ print(sum(i, j));} // NoSuchMethodError
```

The code fails, even though it is type correct. This is of course very common. If one could reliably ensure the correctness of realistic programs by type checking alone, truly statically typed programming languages would have an enormous economic advantage and would in fact be a "silver bullet" for all software bugs.

Our latest variant does contain errors, but it is type safe. Let's take a version that isn't type safe:

```
int i;
int j = 0;
Object sum(Object a, Object b) => a + b; // type warning: a has no method '+'
main(){ print(sum(3, 4));} // prints 7
```

This version works just fine, like our first two variants. However, the type warning is completely justified. According to the type annotations, an invocation like

```
sum(new Object(), []); // NoSuchMethodError
```

is supposed to make sense, but it clearly does not. The type annotations on sum are wrong, but the logic in the actual program is correct. Since type annotations cannot influence semantics, it follows that one can have incorrect annotations and still have a valid running program.

The type annotation on sum() is not quite as absurd as it seems.

```
sum('ab', 'surd'); // evaluates to 'absurd'
```

It turns out that sum() is a useful function on any number of types. Anything that has defined a + method makes sense. It might seem like marking the arguments with type Object is appropriate, as Object is the common super type of all these different types. As we have seen, this is not the case.

The best course of action is this case is to avoid type annotations on sum() altogether. This avoids egregious type warnings. If no type is explicitly given to a variable in the program, the variable's type is **dynamic**. The type **dynamic** is a special type that denotes the fact that the type checker should not complain about operations on the variable or about assignments to/from the variable.

In contrast, explicitly using the type Object means we really expect that any object is a valid value for the variable. The two cases may appear similar, but when we operate on an expression of type Object, we will get warnings if we try to use methods that are not supported by all objects. In contrast, using the type **dynamic** effectively silences static type checking entirely. It tells the typechecker that we believe we know what we're doing. This is useful in many situations where an accurate type is difficult (or impossible) to express.

In principle, one can write **dynamic** as a type annotation explicitly.

dynamic sum(**dynamic** a, **dynamic** b) => a + b; // Never do this!

However, this is pointless and very bad style. It conveys no information to either type checker or human. The absence of a type annotation means exactly the same thing, but without gratuitous clutter.

sum(a, b) => a + b; // So much better

To get a better sense of types and their use, let us return to our old friend Point:

```
class Point {
  num x, y;
  Point(this.x, this.y);
  Point scale(num factor) => new Point(x*factor, y*factor);
  Point operator +(Point p) => new Point(x + p.x, y + p.y);
  static num distance(Point p1, Point p2) {
    num dx = p1.x - p2.x;
    num dy = p1.y - p2.y;
    return sqrt(dx*dx + dy*dy);
  }
}
```

This version is fully annotated with types. Notice that we marked the instance variables with type num rather than int or even double. We chose num because it is the common supertype of integers and doubles, and points work well with coordinates of either type (or even a mixture of the two).

You can also see that the shorthand constructor using initializing formals does not include type annotations. The types of the parameters are derived from the instance variable declarations, so there is no need to repeat them.

5.3 Interface Types

Dart types are interface types. They define a set of methods available on an object. As a general rule, they do not tell us anything about the object's implementation. Once again, this is in keeping with the basic principle that it is the object's behavior that matters, not its pedigree.

Perhaps surprisingly, Dart has no syntax for interface declarations. Interfaces are introduced via class declarations. Each class introduces an implicit interface based on the signatures of its members. Cases that call for a traditional interface declaration are easily handled by defining a purely abstract class.

Any class can implement an interface, even if it has no relation to the class that defines the interface. This is the reason that interface declarations are unnecessary in Dart. We saw an example of such a class, Pair in Section 2.7.

```
abstract class Pair {
  get first;
  get second;
}
```

We can declare implementations of the interface defined by Pair

```
class ArrayPair implements Pair {
  var _rep;
  ArrayPair(a, b) {
    _rep = [a, b];
  }
  get first => _rep[0];
  get second => _rep[1];
}
```

The class ArrayPair implements Pair rather than subclassing it. The **implements** clause is followed by the names of one or more interfaces that the class is intended to implement.

A class does not inherit any implementation from the interfaces named in the **implements** clause. In this particular example, there is no implementation to inherit, but in many cases the distinction matters.

What the **implements** clause does is induce an explicit subtype relationship between the class and the interfaces the clause lists. The subtype relation affects the behavior of the Dart typechecker as well as the runtime.

To see the effects of the subtyping relations induced by the **implements** clause, let's write a function that acts on pairs:

```
Pair reversePair(Pair p) => new ArrayPair(p.second, p.first);
```

We can use reversePair() as follows

```
reversePair(new ArrayPair(3, 4)); // a new Pair, with first = 4 and second = 3
```

The Dart type checker is perfectly happy with this code. However, if we had omitted the **implements** clause, the type checker would not know that ArrayPair is a subtype of Pair. In that case, it would complain both about the definition of reversePair() and about its use. At the definition of reversePair(), it would warn us that the returned object, of type ArrayPair was not a subtype of the declared return type Pair. A similar notification would be issued at the call site because the actual parameter has type ArrayPair whereas the formal parameter is of type Pair.

The type checker will perform such checks at every point where an object is transferred from one variable to another. These value transfers occur when:

- An assignment is performed.

- An actual argument is passed to a function.

- A result is returned from a function.

Each of the interfaces given in the **implements** clause is considered a *direct super-interface* of the class. In our example, Pair is a direct superinterface of ArrayPair. In addition, the immediate superclass of a class is also considered to be one of the classes' direct superinterfaces.

The complete set of *superinterfaces* of a type can be computed by taking the set of direct superinterfaces, and recursively computing and adding the superinterfaces of each. The computation is complete when no new element can be added to the set.

Strictly speaking, the typechecker does not enforce the superinterface relation when checking value transfers. What is checked is *assignability*. Assignability is more liberal than subtyping. Dart considers types assignable if they are subtypes in *either direction.* That is, not only is ArrayPair assignable to Pair (because ArrayPair is a subtype of Pair) but Pair is assignable to ArrayPair. The latter rule may well puzzle you. After all, there could be many implementations of Pair and they would usually not have all the members of ArrayPair. To understand why Dart acts this way, let's look at another example.

```
class Monster {
  // many monstrous features
}


class Vampire extends Monster {
  get bloodType => 'O';
}


Map<String, Monster> monsters = {
  'Frankenstein' : new Monster(),
  'Godzilla' : new Monster(),
  'Dracula' : new Vampire()
}
...
Vampire vamp = monsters['Dracula'];
```

The monster map monsters is only guaranteed to contain instances of Monster. A typical type checker would complain that the result of the lookup on the last line above is a Monster, which is not a subtype of Vampire.

In practice, when we look up the key 'Dracula' in the monster map monsters we know that we're going to get a Vampire back. Such situations arise frequently. Using conventional type checking rules, one would be forced to use casts. Imposing such a burden upon programmers runs counter to Dart's philosophy of using types as a tool to improve the developer experience. Instead, Dart's assignability rules support implicit downcasting.

Of course, this means that Dart's type discipline is unsound. We cannot guarantee that a Dart program that passes the type checker is in fact free of runtime errors. However, as we noted in the tour above, in reality no static type system can do so.

Typically, those properties that a type system can enforce are defined to be part of its purview, while those it cannot are relegated elsewhere. A classic example is pattern matching in functional languages, which defines the enforcement of certain properties to lie outside the static type system.

As we shall see in Section 5.5, there are other reasons why Dart type checking is not sound.

5.4   Types in Action: The Expression Problem, Typed

To get a better sense of types in Dart, let us revisit the expression problem, which we first encountered in Section 2.15.1. We'd like to type check our original solution.

We'll start by adding type information to our evaluator. When typechecking the evaluator we need to know that the mixins for addition and subtraction have fields that support an int valued eval() method, so we annotate the fields with the type ExpressionWithEval. We still have no dependency on other libraries (except dart:core of course). We don't need to know whether ExpressionWithEval is actually a subtype of Expression for example.

We also want to guarantee that the mixin for numbers has a field val of type int, and that all eval methods return integers.

```
library evaluator;

abstract class ExpressionWithEval {
  int get eval;
}

abstract class AdditionWithEval {
  ExpressionWithEval get operand1;
  ExpressionWithEval get operand2;
  int get eval => operand1.eval + operand2.eval;
}

abstract class SubtractionWithEval {
  ExpressionWithEval get operand1;
  ExpressionWithEval get operand2;
  int get eval => operand1.eval - operand2.eval;
}

abstract class NumberWithEval {
  int get val;
  int get eval => val;
}
```

However, when adding types to multiplication_evaluator we find that we need to add an import, because we must access the type ExpressionWithEval. It is not surprising that evaluation code for all types might depend on the type defined in the original evaluator, but it is just a tad regrettable that we can no longer compile these independently.

```
library multiplication_evaluator;
import 'evaluator.dart' show ExpressionWithEval;

abstract class MultiplicationWithEval {
  ExpressionWithEval get operand1;
  ExpressionWithEval get  operand2;
  int get eval => operand1.eval * operand2.eval;
}
```

The code for the string_converter library is annotated much like that of evaluator:

```
library string_converter;

abstract class ExpressionWithStringConversion {
  String toString();
}

abstract class AdditionWithStringConversion {
  ExpressionWithStringConversion get operand1;
  ExpressionWithStringConversion get operand2;
  String toString() => '$operand1 + $operand2';
}


abstract class SubtractionWithStringConversion {
  ExpressionWithStringConversion get operand1;
  ExpressionWithStringConversion get operand2;
  String toString() => '$operand1 - $operand2';
}

abstract class NumberWithStringConversion {
  int get val;
  String toString() => '$val';
}

abstract class MultiplicationWithStringConversion {
  ExpressionWithStringConversion get operand1;
  ExpressionWithStringConversion get operand2;
  String toString() => '$operand1 * $operand2';
}
```

Strictly speaking, since all objects support toString(), we need not have annotated our operands with type ExpressionWithStringConversion or even defined ExpressionWithStringConversion. All that was really required was to note that our toString() methods returned String so we could check that the values being returned from these methods were indeed strings. However, a key goal of types in Dart is clarity, and we want to emphasize that we are using the same pattern as in the evaluator here as well.

The fact that libraries that introduce new functions to the expression hierarchy do not depend on the core class hierarchy also means that one could annotate these libraries with types regardless of whether we chose to add type annotations to the core class hierarchy. Hence, programmers who are fond of type checking can add new functions to the system and type check them even if the designers of the original hierarchy chose not to use types at all.

Now let us annotate the types of fields in our class hierarchy. Doing so requires us to import type Expression.

```
library abstract_expressions;
import 'expressions.dart' show Expression;


abstract class AbstractExpression{}

abstract class AbstractAddition {
  Expression operand1, operand2;
  AbstractAddition(this.operand1, this.operand2);
}

abstract class AbstractSubtraction {
  Expression operand1, operand2;
  AbstractSubtraction(this.operand1, this.operand2);
}

abstract class AbstractNumber {
  int val;
  AbstractNumber(this.val);
}


library multiplication;
import 'expressions.dart' show Expression;


abstract class AbstractMultiplication {
  Expression operand1, operand2;
  AbstractMultiplication(this.operand1, this.operand2);
}
```

The dependency on the expressions library is more unpleasant than the dependency of multiplication_evaluator on evaluator. We had originally defined our core hierarchy completely independently of the final application library. It would seem that adding types is making our code less modular. We shall see how to obtain the desired decoupling while keeping the types when we discuss generics in the next section.

Finally, let's add types to our main library. The only change we need to make is annotate the local variable *e* with the type Expression. The rest of the library is unchanged.

```
main(){
  Expression e = new Multiplication(
                    new Addition(new Number(4), new Number(2)),
                    new Subtraction(new Number(10), new Number(7))
                  );
  print('$e = ${e.eval}');
}
```

Altogether it has been straightforward to add types to our expressions code. The only real issue is that all uses of Expression and its subclasses have to be typechecked against the types defined by the mixin applications. To overcome this issue, we'll need more sophisticated types: generics.

5.5   Generics

Dart classes may be *generic*—that is, they may be parameterized by types.
Generic classes can be given actual type parameters:

```
List<String> l;
Map<String, int> m;
```

Types like these are called *parameterized types*.

Providing type parameters to a generic class is not required however. If one chooses to use the name of a generic class without type arguments, the type **dynamic** is used implicitly in place of all missing type arguments. So one can write

```
List l;
Map m;
```

and this would be fully equivalent to

```
List<dynamic> l;
Map<dynamic, dynamic> m;
```

Obviously, the former, more concise form is preferred. It is bad style to clutter the code with types that convey no new information. There are, however, situations where writing the type **dynamic** explicitly is desirable, as in

```
Map<String, dynamic> m;
```

If one provides the wrong number of type arguments, all type arguments are disregarded.

```
Map<String> m; // Map
List<String, num> // List
Object<int> // Object
```

The above three examples will each result in a static warning. Aside from the warning, the above are treated as Map, List and Object respectively, which are, as noted above, equivalent to Map<**dynamic**, **dynamic**>, List<**dynamic**> and Object.

Suppose we have

```
class Fruit {
  var color;
  Fruit(this.color);
}


class Apple extends Fruit {
  Apple():super('Red');
}


class Orange extends Fruit {
  Orange():super('Orange');
}

// print colors of all fruits in a list
printColors(List<Fruit> fruits) {
  for (Fruit f in fruits) print(f.color);
}


main() {
  List<Apple> apples =  <Apple>[];
  List<Orange> oranges =  new List<Orange>();
  apples.add(new Apple());
  oranges..add(new Orange())
         ..add(new Orange());
  printColors(apples); // prints Red once
  printColors(oranges); // prints Orange twice
}
```

We have two classes, Apple and Orange both of which are subclasses of Fruit. We have a simple function, printColors() that takes lists of Fruit and prints the color of each member in the list. We can use this function with apples or oranges because both are lists of Fruit. This is intuitive—if Apple is a Fruit, surely a List<Apple> is a List<Fruit>?

If you've ever delved into the strange world of generic types, you realize that life can be a lot more complicated. Nevertheless, in Dart, it is indeed the case that a List<Apple> is a List<Fruit>.

More generally, if G is a generic class with n type parameters, then if S_i is a subtype of T_i for $i \in 1..n$, then $G < S_1, \ldots, S_n ><: G < T_1, \ldots, T_n >$, where $T <: S$ indicates that T is a subtype of S.

This behavior is known as *covariance*.

It is well known that covariant subtyping of generics is problematic.

```
addApple(List<Fruit> fruits) {
  fruits[fruits.length-1] = new Apple();
}
  addApple(oranges); // now oranges contains an Apple!
```

The sad fact is that the intuitive relation most people expect does not actually hold in an imperative language. This confronts language designers with an unpalatable choice: produce an unsound type system, which means that you cannot rely on it; or go with the rules of logic, leaving most programmers utterly baffled. The author has been through this exercise several times. In Dart, we have deliberately chosen to make the type system unsound.

5.5.1 The Expression Problem with Generics

In our previous iteration over the expression problem (5.4), we found that adding types introduced an undesirable dependency into our class hierarchy libraries; they became dependent upon the leaf type Expression. We shall now see how generics can be used to alleviate this problem.

Our first step is to make the core classes generic, parameterized by E. E represents the final expression type in our application. This gets rid of the dependency on Expression.

```
library abstract_expressions;

abstract class AbstractExpression{}

abstract class AbstractAddition<E> {
  E operand1, operand2;
  AbstractAddition(this.operand1, this.operand2);
}
```

```
abstract class AbstractSubtraction<E> {
  E operand1, operand2;
  AbstractSubtraction(this.operand1, this.operand2);
}


abstract class AbstractNumber {
  int val;
  AbstractNumber(this.val);
}



library multiplication;

abstract class AbstractMultiplication<E> {
  E operand1, operand2;
  AbstractMultiplication(this.operand1, this.operand2);
}
```

We'll also parameterize the mixin classes that represent our functions. In the evaluator mixins, we need a type parameter that is known to be a subtype of Expression-WithEval so that we can invoke the eval method without getting warnings.

```
library evaluator;


abstract class ExpressionWithEval {
  int get eval;
}

abstract class AdditionWithEval<E extends ExpressionWithEval> {
  E get operand1;
  E get operand2;
  int get eval => operand1.eval + operand2.eval;
}

abstract class SubtractionWithEval<E extends ExpressionWithEval>  {
  E get operand1;
  E get operand2;
  int get eval => operand1.eval - operand2.eval;
}

abstract class NumberWithEval  {
  int get val;
  int get eval => val;
}
```

```
library multiplication_evaluator;

import 'evaluator.dart' show ExpressionWithEval;


abstract class MultiplicationWithEval<E extends ExpressionWithEval> {
  E get operand1;
  E get  operand2;
  int get eval => operand1.eval * operand2.eval;
}
```

Similarly, the mixins for string conversion should have E bounded by Expression-WithStringConversion:

```
library string_converter;


abstract class ExpressionWithStringConversion {
  String toString();
}


abstract class AdditionWithStringConversion<E extends ExpressionWithStringConversion> {
  E get operand1;
  E get operand2;
  String toString() => '$operand1 + $operand2';
}


abstract class SubtractionWithStringConversion<E extends ExpressionWithStringConversion> {
  E get operand1;
  E get operand2;
  String toString() => '$operand1 - $operand2';
}

abstract class NumberWithStringConversion {
  int get val;
  String toString() => '$val';
}

abstract class MultiplicationWithStringConversion<E extends ExpressionWithStringConversion> {
  E get operand1;
  E get operand2;
  String toString() => '$operand1 * $operand2';
}
```

Finally, we must modify expressions to instantiate all these parameterized types.

```dart
library expressions;

import 'abstractExpressions.dart' show
        AbstractAddition,
        AbstractExpression,
        AbstractNumber,
        AbstractMultiplication,
        AbstractSubtraction;


import 'evaluator.dart' show
        AdditionWithEval,
        ExpressionWithEval,
        MultiplicationWithEval,
        NumberWithEval,
        SubtractionWithEval;


import 'multiplication.dart';

import 'multiplicationEvaluator.dart';

import 'stringConverter.dart' show
        AdditionWithStringConversion,
        ExpressionWithStringConversion,
        MultiplicationWithStringConversion,
        NumberWithStringConversion,
        SubtractionWithStringConversion;


abstract class Expression = AbstractExpression with
            ExpressionWithEval, ExpressionWithStringConversion;


class Addition = AbstractAddition<Expression> with
        AdditionWithEval<Expression>,
        AdditionWithStringConversion<Expression>
        implements Expression;


class Subtraction = AbstractSubtraction<Expression> with
        SubtractionWithEval<Expression>,
        SubtractionWithStringConversion<Expression>
        implements Expression;
```

```
class Number = AbstractNumber with
               NumberWithEval, NumberWithStringConversion
               implements Expression;


class Multiplication =
    AbstractMultiplication<Expression> with
            MultiplicationWithEval<Expression>,
            MultiplicationWithStringConversion<Expression>
            implements Expression;
```

This concludes our discussion of the expression problem. Remember that the issue of extending a set of type variants and functions upon them is universal, and the patterns shown here can be helpful for many applications that have nothing to do with expressions. The referenced papers by Torgersen[8] and by Zenger and Odersky[9] are highly recommended for those interested in diving deeper.

5.6   Function Types

Function types are treated specially in Dart. All functions implement Function, but function types are compared based on their structure.

The type of a function is based on its return type and on the types of its formal parameters. The type reflects whether the parameters are named or positional, whether the positional parameters are required, and the names of the named parameters.

At this writing, Dart has no syntax for expressing function types, so we will introduce a special notation here. In the simplest case, a function takes n positional parameters, all of whom are required. As a special case, n can be 0. Assuming the formal parameters have types $T_1, \ldots, T_n$ and the return type is T, we can write the function type as $F_t = (T_1, \ldots, T_n) \to T$. For example, we would write the type of

```
num twice(num x) => x * 2;
```

as $(num) \to num$, and the type of

```
num product(List<num> nums) => nums.reduce( (a, b) => a * b);
```

is $(List < num >) \to num$. The type of reduce() itself is interesting, because reduce() is a function that takes a function as its argument. The type of reduce() is $((E, E) \to E) \to E$, where E is the type parameter of List. In our example, nums is a List<num> and so num is substituted for E, so that List<num>.reduce() has the type $((num, num) \to num) \to num$.

However, the type of the actual function argument passed to reduce() is $(\mathbf{dynamic}, \mathbf{dynamic}) \to \mathbf{dynamic}$.

This is a perfectly valid argument, because (**dynamic**, **dynamic**) → **dynamic** is a subtype of $(num, num) → num$. This makes sense, because the function type accepts arguments of type **dynamic**, which include type num. Its result type is **dynamic**, which is acceptable everywhere.

Suppose we wrote product slightly differently

```
num product(List<num> nums) => nums.reduce( (num a, num b) => a * b);
```

Now the argument to reduce() has type $(num, num) →$ **dynamic**, which is still perfectly valid. Suppose we change the code ever so slightly to

```
num product(List<num> nums) => nums.reduce( (int a, int b) => a * b);
```

The argument of reduce() now has type $(int, int) →$ **dynamic**. So is $(int, int) →$ **dynamic** a subtype of $(num, num) →$ **dynamic**? You might be forgiven for thinking so—after all, int is a subtype of num. Alas, if we were to use this version with a list of numbers that included doubles, reduce() would call its argument function with a double extracted from the list; but doubles are not integers, and double is not assignable to int.

We can now ask what are the general rules for subtyping among functions? Given F_t and another function type $F_s = (S_1, \ldots, S_n) → S$, when can we assume F_t is a subtype of F_s?

Type theory tells us that this only holds if T is a subtype of S and if, for $i \in 1..n$, S_i is a subtype of T_i. That is, the type of each formal parameter of F_s must be a subtype of the corresponding formal in F_t. Notice that the direction of the subtyping relation is *reversed*. This phenomenon is known as *contravariance*. The logic is inescapable. Suppose we pass a function f of type F_t to a function $h(g)$. If the formal parameter g has type F_s, it may be safely passed actual parameters that are subtypes of the S_i. It follows that each of the formal parameters of f of type T_i must accept any subtype of S_i, and so T_i must be a *supertype* of S_i.

Unfortunately this reasoning, while unassailable, runs counter to the intuitions of almost everyone. Experience shows that reasoning about the types of higher order functions is difficult. Dart deliberately seeks to avoid confronting the programmer with such complex types as much as possible.

As we have already noted, type soundness is not a goal of Dart. So it seems natural to abandon it and conform to the common (if incorrect) intuition and adopt a *covariant* rule, which would state that F_t is a subtype of F_s if T is a subtype of S and T_i is subtype to S_i for $i \in 1..n$. In fact, Dart's rule is somewhat different.

Recall that the intuition behind the subtype rules for function types is based on what constitutes a valid invocation of a function valued parameter g to a higher-order function h. For ordinary (non-function) objects, parameter passing is governed by the assignability rule, which allows subtyping in either direction. Hence, when g is invoked with actual arguments, their types are only required to be assignable to the formal parameters of g. Any argument must have a type assignable to the appropriate S_i, and so it must be assignable to T_i. In other words, the argument can be either a subtype of T_i or a supertype of T_i. Hence, it is acceptable if T_i is either a subtype or a subtype of S_i. We therefore assume that F_t is a subtype of F_s if T is assignable to S and T_i is assignable to S_i.

So far so good. The rule above, while unsound, is very liberal. Programmers who run afoul of it are indeed likely to be passing a function whose parameters have types completely unrelated to the formal parameter.

We still have to account for optional and named parameters.

5.6.1 Optional Positional Parameters

As a first step, let us extend our notation for function types to accommodate optional positional parameters. A function might have k optional positional parameters. We'll write them after the required parameters, inside square brackets, echoing the syntax used in function signatures: $(T_1, \ldots, T_n, [T_{n+1}, \ldots, T_{n+k}]) \to T$.

We can safely pass a function that takes optional parameters to contexts where those parameters are required. The function can accept them. The converse situation is unacceptable. A function that requires certain parameters cannot be used in a context where they are deemed optional, since they may not in fact be provided. The subtype must be able to accept at least as many parameters as the supertype. However, not all of the subtype's parameters need be required parameters; in fact, it's fine if none of them are required.

This leads us to the actual rule:

A function type $F_t = (T_1, \ldots, T_n, [T_{n+1}, \ldots, T_{n+k}]) \to T$ is a subtype of a function type $F_s = (S_1, \ldots, S_j, [S_{j+1}, \ldots, S_m]) \to S$ iff:

1. $j \geq n$ and $m \leq n + k$.

2. $\forall i \in 1..m, T_i$ is assignable to S_i.

3. Either S is **void** or T is assignable to S.

The subtype requires n parameters, whereas the supertype has j required parameters. When a function f_t of type F_t is used in a place that requires type F_s, it will always be passed at least j parameters. Since F_t requires n parameters, the first item insists that $j \geq n$, so f_t is guaranteed to get as many parameters as it requires. The maximum number of parameters that might be passed is m, the total number of parameters of F_s. The function f_t will accept up to $n + k$ parameters—n required and k optional. As long as m is no larger than $n + k$, the number of parameters passed will be acceptable to f_t. The types of the actual arguments must be assignable to the formals of f_t. Since at most m actuals will in fact be sent, we only require assignability for the first m parameter types.

The last item is a twist we've neglected so far. Dart allows you to identify functions that are not intended to return a result. These can be marked using the special return type **void**. If F_s returns **void**, the type checker assumes the result is not used, and so it has no significance.

5.6.2   Named Parameters

What of named parameters? Again, let's introduce some notation for the types of
functions with named parameters. We will describe named parameters between braces
similar to Dart map literals, again echoing the concrete syntax used in function signatures. The named parameters appear after the positional ones. Each named parameter
will be denoted by a type followed by its name.

As a concrete example we'll look at the method firstWhere() of Iterable.

```
E firstWhere(bool test(E value), {E orElse()});
```

which has type $((E) \rightarrow bool, \{() \rightarrow E \text{ orElse}\}) \rightarrow E$.

The firstWhere() method takes a predicate as an argument, just like where(). Instead
of returning a collection of results for which the predicate holds, firstWhere() simply
returns the first such element.

A close relative of firstWhere() is lastWhere() which returns the last element for which
the predicate holds.

```
E lastWhere(bool test(E value), {E orElse()});
```

So the general form of a function type with named arguments is

$$(T_1, \ldots, T_n, \{T_{x_1}x_1, \ldots, T_{x_k}x_k\}) \rightarrow T$$

Let us consider the subtyping rules for such function types. Since named parameters
are always optional, a logic similar to what we used in the last subsection applies. We
can pass a function that takes named parameters to a context that does not specify
named parameters as long as its return type and required parameters are acceptable.

If the formal parameter does specify named parameters we must ensure that the
incoming argument accepts all of the named parameters mentioned in the supertype; it
can also accept additional ones. Notice that we make no mention of optional positionals
here. In Dart, a function cannot have both optional positional parameters and named
parameters.

We can state these rules formally as follows:

A function type $F_t = (T_1, \ldots, T_n, \{T_{x_1}x_1, \ldots, T_{x_k}x_k\}) \rightarrow T$ is a subtype of a function
type $F_s = (S_1, \ldots, S_n, \{S_{y_1}y_1, \ldots, S_{y_m}y_m\}) \rightarrow S$ iff:

1. Either S is **void** or T is assignable to S.

2. $\forall i \in 1..n, T_i$ is assignable to S_i.

3. $k \geq m$ and $y_i \in \{x_1, \ldots, x_k\}, i \in 1..m$.

4. For all $y_i \in \{y_1, \ldots, y_m\}, y_i = x_j \Rightarrow T_{x_j}$ is assignable to S_{y_i}.

5.6.3   Call() Revisited

In Section 4.6.1 we mentioned that any class that declares the special method name **call**
implicitly implements Function. We can now refine our understanding of the behavior
of **call**.

Suppose we wanted to define a class of maps that also behave as functions from the keys of the map to its values. We'll restrict this to maps from strings to numbers.

```
class MapFunction implements Map<String, num> {
    MapFunction(this._map);
    Map<String, num> _map;
    num operator [](String k) => _map[k];
    void operator []= (String k,  num v) { _map[k] = v;}
    // more map wrapping functions
    num call(String key) => _map[key];
}
```

Instances of class MapFunction are created by passing a map object to the class' constructor. The class then forwards all calls in the Map interface to the map object it wraps. In addition, the **call** method takes an object, uses it as a key into the underlying map and returns the result of the lookup.

Dart ensures not only that MapFunction is considered to implement Function, but that it is considered a subtype of $String \rightarrow num$.

In general, when a class FunctionWannabe declares a call() method, the signature of that method describes a function type F. FunctionWannabe is considered to be a subtype of F. Above we showed this for $F = String \rightarrow num$ and $FunctionWannabe = MapFunction$.

5.7   Type Reification

While type annotations have no presence at runtime, other aspects of types do. As we have already seen, each object carries with it its *runtime type* which can be accessed dynamically via the runtimeType method inherited from Object. Users are free to override runtimeType which means that the implementation type of an object is not, in general, observable via calls to runtimeType.

Each type declaration introduces a compile-time constant object of class Type representing it. These objects are available at runtime as well. Moreover, one can test whether an object is a member of a type via dynamic type tests and type casts, as shown below.

5.7.1   Type Tests

Type tests are expressions that test whether an object belongs to a type

```
var v = [1, 2, 3];
v is List; // true
v is Map; // false
v is Object; // POINTLESS: always true
```

The general form of a type test is e **is** T where e is an expression and T is a type. The type test evaluates e and tests the dynamic type of the result against the type T. The last line in the above code snippet is something that should never appear in a normal Dart program. It will always evaluate to true, because all Dart values are objects.

Because a Dart class can implement an unrelated type, an object may emulate another type T even if the class of the object is not a subclass of T. However, an object cannot completely hide its implementation type, because one can detect it using a type test. This is arguably a violation of the principle that only the behavior of an object should matter. The same argument holds for casts, described below.

5.7.2   Type Casts

Type casts also evaluate an expression and test whether the resulting object belongs to a type, but they are not a predicate. Instead, the cast will throw a CastError if the test fails; otherwise it returns the object unchanged.

```
Object o = [3, 4, 5];
o as List; // a somewhat costly no-op
o as Map; // throws
```

A cast is pretty much a shorthand for

```
var t = e;
t is T ? t : throw new CastError();
```

A typical use of casts might be to validate data

```
List l = readNextVal() as List;
  // I'm pretty sure I'll get a list back from readNextVal()
  // if not, things are really hosed and I should fail
  // Next, do stuff with a list
```

One should be careful not to abuse casts. Consider

```
Object o = [5, 6, 7];
... // lots of intervening logic
o.length; // works; type warning: objects don't always have length
```

Many programmers may be tempted to rewrite the code into

```
Object o = [5, 6, 7];
... // same intervening logic
(o as List).length; // BAD! The wrong way to avoid a warning
```

Casts are executed at runtime and therefore come with runtime cost. If your goal is simply to silence the type checker, just use an assignment:

```
Object o = [5, 6, 7];
... // same intervening logic
List l = o;
l.length;
```

The above works well because of the assignability rule (5.3). Some programmers might object to this idiom because they find it difficult to keep coming up with names for variables. A simple solution is to append a variant of the cast syntax to the variable name:

```
Object o = [5, 6, 7];
... // same intervening logic
List o_as_List = o;
l.length;
```

5.7.3 Checked Mode

During development, it is often very useful to validate the types of variables. For example, we'd like to ensure that incoming parameters or an object returned from a call meet expectations. Dart provides *checked mode* for this purpose. In checked mode, every value transfer is dynamically checked. This means that a dynamic type test is performed automatically for you every time a parameter is passed, a result is returned from a method or function, and on every assignment executed. Checked mode ensures that the dynamic value being assigned to a variable is a member of the static type of the variable being assigned to. Likewise, the dynamic type of an actual parameter is tested against the formal parameter's static type, and the dynamic type of a function's result is tested against the declared return type of the function.

```
num n = 3.0;
int i = n; // dynamic error in checked mode; works in production
num x = i; // always works
int j = null; // always allowed
```

Checked mode's behavior differs from the static type checking rules. When assignments are checked statically, we use the assignability rule (5.3) that permits the assignment if a subtype relation holds in either direction. The dynamic check implemented by checked mode insists that the actual type of the value being assigned is either a subtype of the static type of the variable, or **null**.

We can see this difference in the assignment to i above. The assignment will not cause a static type warning, but does fail in checked mode.

In the absence of checked mode, one could insert typecasts into code, but that would be undesirable. The casts are not only tedious; they introduce runtime overhead, so their systemic use is prohibitively expensive in production. Type casts should be used only when truly necessary.

As you can see, in checked mode, type annotations will impact program behavior; however, this is a developer tool explicitly under programmer control for the purpose of verifying the correctness of the type annotations. Indeed, in checked mode, type annotations act like assertions. Checked mode also activates any **assert** statements in the program (6.2.7).

5.7.4 Reified Generics

Type arguments are reified at runtime. When a generic class is instantiated, the actual type arguments provided are in fact passed at runtime and stored. Thus, the class of an instance created with **new** List<String>() is in fact different from the class of an instance created via **new** List<Object>().

We can write

```
var l = new List<String>();
l is List<String>; // true
l is List<int>; // false
```

One must understand the limitations of such tests in Dart however. Because the type system is unsound there is no hard guarantee that an object that claims to be, say, a List<int> contains only integers. We can be confident that the object is a list, and that it was created as a list of integers. However, any kind of object could subsequently have been inserted into it.

In checked mode however, we have a lot more confidence. Any attempt to corrupt the list by inserting an inappropriate object into it would be trapped in checked mode. Checked mode tests the actual type of objects against the declared types of variables and function results; but in a generic type, the actual type arguments to the generic are substituted for any type variables in the declared types. So, given that List defines

```
operator [int index]= (E e)
```

when one writes

```
var l = new List<String>();
l[0] = 'abc'; // always ok
l[1] = 42; // fails in checked mode - 42 is an int which is not a subtype of String
```

checked mode will ensure that uses of an instance of a generic class cannot be corrupted.

5.7.5 Reification and Optional Typing

How does the concept of optional typing fit in with type reification? In particular, optional types are not supposed to influence runtime semantics, and yet reification clearly does. However, reification only impacts behavior when the program explicitly attempts to observe or determine runtime type structure. These situations are:

- Asking an object for its type, using a type test, cast or a call to runtimeType.

- Setting the runtime type of an object by passing actual type parameters to the constructor of a generic type.

- Using reflection to check or set the type of a variable or function.

- Using checked mode.

- Determining the reified type of a function object via annotations on its signature.

The final three points all have the potential to be impacted by type annotations, which normally have no semantic effect. Of these, the last point is perhaps the most subtle one. If logic depends on a type test involving a function, it can be influenced by a type annotation. The function could be a closure defined explicitly or extracted as a property. The following code demonstrates the issue:

```
typedef int IntFunction(int);

observeAnnotations(f) {
    return f is IntFunction;
}

String id1(String x) => x;
id2(x) => x;
int id3(int x) => x;

observeAnnotations(id1); // false
observeAnnotations(id2); // true
observeAnnotations(id3); // true
```

All three functions id1, id2, id3 are the same except for their type annotations, but they differ in their behavior with respect to type tests due to the type annotations used. Of course, we are already performing a type test explicitly, so it is not that surprising that types should have an effect on behavior in this case.

5.7.6   Types and Proxies

Being able to define transparent proxies for any sort of object is an important property. There is an inherent tension between proxying and typing. Consider our general purpose proxy class Proxy introduced in Section 2.10.

Assume the proxy is emulating type Point. The first difficulty we run into is when we use an instance of Proxy as the value of a typed variable or parameter.

```
Point pointProxy = new Proxy(new Point(0,0)); // warning
```

Since Proxy is neither a subtype nor supertype of Point, the code causes a warning. The best solution is to declare proxyPoint as a dynamically typed variable.

```
var pointProxy = new Proxy(new Point(0,0));
```

Of course, at this point we have lost certain benefits of type checking. If we want to type check our use of pointProxy we'll need another approach. It might seem that all we need to do is add

```
Point pointImposter = pointProxy;
```

but this turns out to be insufficient. While this does silence the static warning, we will run into trouble with dynamic type checks. If we were to write any of the following

```
pointImposter is Point; // false!
pointImposter as Point; // exception!
```

our pretense that our proxy object is a point will be exposed. While we might choose to forego type checking and avoid these situation, in reality we may have to pass pointProxy or pointImposter to code written by others that assumes it works on points. In that case it is quite likely that dynamic tests like the above will occur. Moreover, when running in checked mode, failures will occur the moment one tries to perform assign, pass or return pointProxy to a context that is annotated with type Point.

```
Point pointProxy = new Proxy(new Point(0,0)); // dies in checked mode
```

If we are to engage in any kind of type checking, we need to define a *type-specific proxy*:

```
class PointProxy extends Proxy  implements Point {
  PointProxy(forwardee): super(forwardee);
}
```

Now we can use our proxies reliably:

```
Point pointProxy = new PointProxy(new Point(0,0));
pointProxy is Point; // true!
pointProxy as Point; // identical to pointProxy
```

But wait! There are no methods for x, y, rho, theta, + and so on in PointProxy. Won't we get warnings that PointProxy doesn't implement the Point interface correctly? As it happens, Dart has a special rule that lets us suppress such warnings. If a class declares a noSuchMethod() then no complaints about missing members of support interfaces are given, nor are any such warnings given about incorrect signatures of such members.

The need for type-specific proxies is disappointing. Here, most of the work is done by Proxy but we still have to define per-interface subclasses. This solution is much easier and more maintainable than defining an exhaustive set of forwarding methods, which is what you would have to in a traditionally typed setting, but not as easy as just defining a single Proxy class. In a fully dynamic setting, the shared definition of Proxy would suffice.

We considered several alternatives. Having type tests (including those in checked mode) and casts have user-definable behavior would help, but would entail a performance overhead that the design team was not willing to pay.

A related issue is emulating functions, first introduced in Section 4.6.1. We cannot use the exact same technique as above however, since we cannot implement a specific function type. However, there is an alternative.

The problem arises in practice in Dart's unit test framework. The framework defines a method expectAsync() which takes an asynchronous function and wraps it in a proxy so it appears to be synchronous. The framework needs to work with target functions of various types and arities.

We want the function proxy to have the same signature as its target to avoid any difficulties with dynamic type tests. If we knew the precise function signature we sought to emulate, we could define a suitable **call** method, which would automatically make our proxy class a member of the corresponding function type.

In addition, we need to be able to forward calls from the proxy to its target. Again, this needs to work for varying arities.

A pragmatic solution relies on the fact that we can realistically limit the arity of the functions involved to some fixed value n. Assume $n = 5$ for the sake of our examples, but if that is insufficient one can choose $n = 10$ or $n = 255$ or whatever value suits—the principle is the same. We will also ignore the possibility of using named arguments. In this case, we can define **call** to take five optional parameters. This makes our proxy a member of the type ([**dynamic, dynamic, dynamic, dynamic, dynamic**]) $\rightarrow$ **dynamic** which is a subtype of any function with no more than five required arguments and no named arguments. As a result, the proxy object not only supports the same legal calls as its target, but operates safely even with respect to type tests, casts and in checked mode.

It remains to define the code in our **call** method to forward calls to the target. Our implementation needs to determine the proper number of arguments to pass along. Assuming the call to the proxy function has the correct arity, we need to determine how many arguments were in fact passed to us, and then call the target with those.

To accomplish this, we set the default value for each argument to a special marker object. Since default parameter values must be constant in Dart, the marker object is a compile-time constant object. We can then define the argument list conveniently as a list literal with all formal parameters, filtering out all occurrences of our marker value using the removeWhere() method on lists. We can then use Function.apply(), which we first saw in Section 4.6, to forward the call. Here is the necessary code

```
class UnsentArgumentMarker{
  const UnsentArgumentMarker();
}
const NO_ARG = const UnsentArgumentMarker();
class ProxyForFunctionOfArity5 implements Function {
  Function target;
  ProxyForFunctionOfArity5(this.target);
  call([a0 = NO_ARG, a1 = NO_ARG, a2 = NO_ARG, a3 = NO_ARG, a4 = NO_ARG]){
    List args = [a0, a1, a2, a3, a4]..removeWhere((arg) => arg == NO_ARG);
    return Function.apply(target, args);
  }
}
```

The real code in the unit test framework has some extra logic to deal with handling asynchrony, but that is not our concern here. We could filter out the unsent arguments in other ways, but this code is elegant and concise at some slight expense in efficiency. What is important to note here is how we have emulated a broad set of function types and the technique of determining which arguments were actually passed along.

Dart's type system makes one more special dispensation for proxies. The annotation (7.3) @proxy has special significance to the type system. If a class is annotated with @proxy, then the Dart analyzer will refrain from issuing warnings when a method is accessed on an instance of the class, even if the class is not statically known to support such a method.

5.8   Malformed Types

What happens if we annotate a variable with a type that does not exist? According to the principles we've elucidated above, the code should function unchanged except in checked mode.

```
UndefinedType v = 91;
```

Assuming UndefinedType is in fact undefined, Dart will issue a warning. In checked mode, the assignment to v will cause a runtime error when the system tries to check that int is a subtype of UndefinedType. However

```
UndefinedType v = null;
```

won't cause any errors at runtime, because no subtype test is performed when the value being assigned to a variable is **null**.

Undefined types may arise due to varied causes: typographical errors, forgotten imports or as a result of mentioning a type before actually defining it. In some cases, the name used in a type annotation might denote a function or variable. In any case where the name does not denote an actual type declaration, we have a *malformed type*.

Undefined types are a particular form of malformed types. Ambiguous types—types whose meaning is not well specified because different declarations of the same name were imported into the same scope—are also malformed.

Genericity may give rise to malformed types as well. If the generic itself is malformed, any invocation of the generic is malformed as well:

```
UndefinedGeneric<int> ugi; // malformed
UndefinedGeneric  ug; // malformed
```

Finally, type variables are considered malformed when they are referred to in the declaration of a static member:

```
class C<T, S> {
    static T cantReferToTypeVars; // warning
    static S alsoCantReferToTypeVars(T t) { // two warnings here
        S local;  // another here
```

```
      return new Map[T, S](); //and two here
      }
  }
```

Type variables have potentially distinct values for each instance of a generic class. They have no meaning when no instance is involved. It would be possible to simply consider type variables out of scope in static member declarations, but by treating them as in-scope but malformed, Dart can provide better error messages.

The declaration of cantReferToTypeVars gives a warning because T is malformed; it only has meaning in the context of an instance of C. The method alsoCantReferTo-TypeVars will yield multiple warnings: its return type S is malformed, as is the type of its formal parameter. The local variable local also gives rise to a warning, and the instantiation of Map in the final statement of the method yields separate warnings for S and T.

Once a warning has been issued about an occurrence of a malformed type, the static type checker replaces the occurrence with **dynamic** to prevent a pointless cascade of secondary warnings. For example, if we call alsoCantReferToTypeVars, we won't get any warnings:

```
int i =  C.alsoCantReferToTypeVars('abc');
```

There is no point in bombarding the programmer with warnings that are not actionable. One could not make the call correct by changing the type of the variable i or the type of the argument. The problem is at the declaration of C.alsoCantReferToTypeVars, not at any call site.

Similarly, the instantiation of Map<T, S> above gives rise to warnings that T and S are malformed, but not to complaints that they are inappropriate type arguments to Map. We replace the malformed type arguments with **dynamic**, and so produce a Map<**dynamic**, **dynamic**>. We see that using a malformed type as a type argument in a parameterized type does not make the parameterized type malformed. The malformed type argument is instead replaced with **dynamic** which is the type argument used at runtime.

```
List<UndefinedType> l = <int>[3];  // warning, but works even in checked mode
List<int> list = <UndefinedType>[3];  // warning, but works even in checked mode
```

Here, the type of l is taken to be of List<**dynamic**>. A warning is issued that UndefinedType is not defined, but not about any mismatch between the types of the value and the variable. At runtime, checked mode will find that List<int> is a subtype of List<**dynamic**> and so the assignment does not cause a failure.

In the second line, the situation is reversed. The object being assigned is given type List<**dynamic**> because the malformed type UndefinedType is replaced by **dynamic**. Consequently, the object can be assigned to a List<int> (once again showing the unsoundness of generics).

5.9   Unsoundness

We are now in a position to review the various sources of unsoundness in the Dart type system. These are:

- Covariance of generics.

- Downcasting in the assignability rule (5.3).

- Assignability in function types.

- The interaction of privacy and interface types.

We discussed the first two points in Sections 5.3 and 5.5 respectively. The third point is really a product of the first two. Function types are naturally covariant in their return types but contravariant in their argument types. The same reasoning that dictated the use of covariance for generics applies to function types. This alone would make function subtyping an additional source of unsoundness.

In addition, the rules for assignability apply to all value transfers, including passing in function arguments and returning function results, which dictates the use of assignability for both argument and return types as discussed in Section 5.6.

The final source of unsoundness in Dart is one that we have not yet discussed—the interaction of ADT style privacy at the library level with interface-based types. To understand this interaction, let's look at a variation on the stack example from the previous chapter. In this version, we will implement a class **Stack** so that we can instantiate multiple stacks:

```
library stack3;

class Stack {
  List _contents = [];
  get isEmpty => _contents.isEmpty;
  get top => isEmpty ? throw 'Cannot get top of empty stack' : _contents.last;
  get pop => isEmpty? throw 'Cannot pop empty stack' : _contents.removeLast();
  push(e) {
    _contents.add(e);
    return e;
  }
}

clone(Stack s) {
  Stack ns = new Stack();
  ns._contents = new List.from(s._contents);
  return ns;
}
```

We've added a clone function that takes a stack and produces another one with the same contents. This isn't really a good idea, but it will suit our purpose here. Something that should raise a red flag is the fact that clone accesses the private variable _contents of its formal parameter s. This is quite natural in a language that is designed around the notion of abstract data types (ADTs). In such a language, we are assured by the type system that any incoming parameter will be an instance of the class Stack that we have defined, and so will have a field named _contents.

And therein lies the rub: Dart is not designed around the notion of abstract data types. Dart is designed around the notion of interfaces. A type in Dart never denotes a specific implementation type. Rather, it denotes the interface of such a type. Anyone can implement the type Stack, and the implementation can be entirely different from the one defined in the class Stack. In particular, the implementation might not have a _contents field.

Indeed, suppose we decide to produce an alternative implementation of Stack on another library.

```
library stack4;

import 'stack3.dart' as stack show clone, Stack;

class Stack4 implements stack.Stack {
  final List _array = [];
  get isEmpty => _array.isEmpty;
  get top => isEmpty ? throw 'Cannot get top of empty stack' : _array.last;
  get pop => isEmpty? throw 'Cannot pop empty stack' : _array.removeLast();
  push(e) {
    _array.add(e);
    return e;
  }
}


main() {
  stack.clone(new Stack4());
}
```

Clearly, the call to stack.clone() will fail with a NoSuchMethodError when we try to access the non-existent _contents getter on the incoming parameter, which is an instance of Stack4 and indeed has no such getter. The question is whether the type system should complain about this code.

In a system based on ADTs, we might complain that Stack4 does not implement
stack.Stack because it lacks the _contents accessor. This raises several difficulties:

- Since _contents is private to stack, its very existence must not be made known to
  other libraries. In particular, generating warnings in implementors of an interface
  is unacceptable. Adding a private member should be a purely internal decision of a
  class. If adding a private member to a class would spawn warnings in implementors
  of the class, this would not be possible.

- Setting the preceding objection aside, suppose we did issue a warning? What is
  the developer working on Stack4 to do? Defining a _contents accessor in Stack4 will
  not satisfy the requirement, because it is private to stack4 and cannot be accessed
  outside. The call inside clone will fail in exactly the same way. The _contents
  members in stack3 and stack4 are different. In short, no one outside stack3.Stack
  can ever implement a _contents getter that will implement the accessor defined
  inside stack3.

An alternative approach is to complain inside clone(). A variable of type Stack
cannot reliably be assumed to have a private accessor such as _contents. Unfortunately,
this would imply that no private instance members could ever be used on any object
except **this**. Object-based encapsulation enforces this alternative. As we discussed in
the previous chapter, Dart explicitly rejects object-based encapsulation.

In reality, no warnings are issued anywhere, and so again the system is unsound.
This unsoundness is a direct consequence of the fact that the privacy discipline is based
on ADTs whereas typing is based purely on interfaces.

Dart gives the programmer the option of defining abstract data types, in which case
they must clearly document that the abstract types they are defining should not be
implemented by others (though they can be extended by subclasses). One can define a
single abstract datatype or a number of cooperating types in this style.

Alternatively, the programmer may opt to work in the preferred, interface based
style, in which case private members should only be accessed via **this**, effectively following object-based encapsulation.

5.10   Related Work

The rigidity of type systems has provoked many attempts to relax it. In Scheme, a
great deal of research was conducted on soft-typing, which was tied to type inference.
More recent efforts in Racket mix typed and untyped code but at a relatively coarse
granularity. Each module is either typed or untyped. Data crossing the boundaries between the typed and untyped units is dynamically checked. These checks are somewhat
reminiscent of checked mode.

Dart's optional type scheme is most closely related to the one developed by Strongtalk[16].
However, in Dart, optional typing is more tightly integrated into the language. Strongtalk
did not reify generics and did not have a checked mode. Furthermore, warnings were the

exclusive province of the IDE; compilation was completely independent of typechecking. Finally, Strongtalk had a sound type system with declaration side variance for generics.

The term *optional typing* was used in the context of Common Lisp, but denoted a somewhat different idea. Types were treated as valid assertions by the compiler, which leveraged them for optimization. However, these type annotations were not validated, making the system inherently unsafe. Dart requires pointer safety and implementations are not allowed to trust type annotations.

Dart's mix of unsound generics and reification is unusual. The influence of Beta[17], where genericity is also covariant is clear. However, generics in Beta are not a special feature but instead are modeled by nested type members and so explicitly reified. In contrast, mainstream languages like Java and C# use sound type systems that include variance declarations. In Java, generics are not reified and variance is use based, whereas in C# generics are reified and variance is declaration based. Older designs such as C++ and Modula-3 use template-based expansion mechanisms.

5.11 Summary

Dart types are based on the concept of interfaces rather than implementation. Every class induces an interface that can be implemented by other classes, even if their implementations are unrelated.

Dart supports optional typing. Typed and untyped code may be freely intermixed. Dart type annotations do not effect runtime behavior, but uses of reified types naturally do. Dart, quite deliberately, does not have a sound type system. Instead, type rules are designed heuristically to balance flexibility and safety in the interests of developer productivity. Violations of the type rules lead to warnings that may be selectively disabled. Type warnings never preclude compilation and execution of the program.

During development, the use of checked mode allows type annotations to be interpreted as assertions, introducing dynamic type checks.

Dart includes generic types, which are treated covariantly. Generics and superinterface declarations are reified and can be tested at runtime.

Chapter 6

Expressions and Statements

Expressions and statements are the backbone of most programming languages. We have seen many of Dart's expressions and statements already. In this chapter we will give a systematic overview of the expressions and statements of Dart.

6.1 Expressions

6.1.1 Literals

We've encountered all of Dart's literals by now, but this is an opportunity to go through them all in an orderly fashion.

6.1.1.1 Integers

God made the integers; all the rest is the work of man.

— Leopold Kronecker

In Dart, integers can be of arbitrary size. However, the use of very large integers is likely to be relatively expensive. Beyond a certain boundary, which varies among implementations, integers can no longer directly take advantage of the underlying hardware representation. Consequently, operations on such large integers become significantly more costly.

The implementation is free to use instances of various classes to implement integers. The only requirement is that any such class implements the built in class int. In practice, different classes are likely to be used depending on the size of the integers represented.

When one asks an integer for its runtimeType, the answer is always int, which is also the type the static checker ascribes to integer literals. Therefore, the only way to discover the underlying implementation class of an integer is through reflection, as discussed in the next chapter.

Integer objects are considered identical if they represent the same mathematical value.

A further complication arises in Dart implementations that compile into Javascript. In Javascript, all numbers are represented as IEEE doubles; there are no integers. As a result, it is prohibitively expensive to implement integer semantics on top of Javascript.[1]

---

1. One can only hope that in due course, Javascript will discover the integers.

On such an implementation, integers will be approximated when they lie outside a given range (an absolute value of approximately 2^{53}).

You can't define subclasses of int, and you cannot have another class implement int. These restrictions are a compromise that allows Dart implementations to provide high performance at the expense of the principle that one should be able to subclass or implement any class.

6.1.1.2   Doubles

Doubles are objects that implement 64-bit floating point numbers in accordance with the IEEE 754 standard. Doubles are instances of the class double in dart:core.

The rules for identity of doubles are subtly different than the rules for equality. Simply put, two doubles are identical if the underlying bit patterns representing the floating point value is the same. For the most part, this means that two doubles are identical iff they are equal, but there are two exceptions:

1. The doubles -0.0 and 0.0 are equal but not identical.

2. A NaN (Not a Number) is identical to itself, but not equal.

You can't define subclasses of double and you cannot have another class implement double. The same rule holds num, for the common supertype of double and int.

6.1.1.3   Booleans

There are exactly two Boolean objects: **true** and **false**. They are members of the class bool.

Unlike some languages, one cannot coerce an arbitrary expression to a Boolean value. If you try to write

```
var x = someComputation();
...
if (x) print(x.foo()); // Don't do this !
```

expecting that the language will turn a non-null value into **true**, you will be disappointed. Remember, Dart frowns on built-in coercions. If x is **true**, the print will execute as expected. However, if x is any other object, it will be treated as **false** in production mode and nothing will be printed. In checked mode it will fail. So the best thing to do is to write proper predicates when performing tests:

```
if (x != null) print(x.foo());
```

This makes it clear to the reader what you are actually testing for and does not rely on coercions, which can be very problematic. Of course, if x really is a Boolean value, it is perfectly fine to write

```
if (x) print(x.foo());
```

In short, **true** is the one and only truth in Dart.

You may well ask why, given our avowed aversion to coercions, do we allow other non-Boolean objects to be treated as **false**? If we were assured that Dart would always run on a Dart VM, we could probably enforce the consistent use of Booleans in all tests. However, given the constraints of compilation to Javascript it turns out to be too costly to insist on using real Boolean values at all times. It is one of the cases where Dart makes a pragmatic compromise.

You can't define subclasses of bool and you cannot have another class implement bool.

6.1.1.4   Strings

String literals can take several forms in Dart. They can be delimited by either single or double quotes:

```
'And I quote: "Strings delimited by single quotes can contain double quotes"'
"And I quote: 'Strings delimited by double quotes can contain single quotes'"
```

Typically, users don't have to remember which quote marks are used to delimit a string. Either way works, making the language a little bit easier to learn. Also, when quotes appear in strings, dealing with them is also simpler, as the examples above show. Naturally, the delimiters have to match—you cannot start a string with a single quote and close it with a double quote for example.

```
'An invalid string" // Illegal! will not parse
"Another invalid string' // Just as illegal
```

Ordinary strings are limited to a single line. If you need a string that covers multiple lines, you can use a *multiline string*. Multiline strings are delimited with triple quotes; again these may be either triple sets of single quotes or triple sets of double quotes.

```
'''And I quote:
"Strings delimited by single quotes
can contain double quotes"
'''

"""And I quote:
'Strings delimited by double quotes
can contain single quotes'
"""
```

There is also another option, which is to split your string into pieces and write the individual pieces next to each other:

```
' "And I quote: '
'Strings delimited by single quotes'
' can contain double quotes"'
```

Dart will implicitly concatenate adjacent strings. The resulting string will not span multiple lines however.

Dart supports a variety of escape sequences within a string. These include

- \n for newline.

- \r for carriage return.

- \f for form feed.

- \b for backspace.

- \t for tab.

- \v for vertical tab.

- \u{h}, where h is a sequence of hexadecimal digits, for the unicode scalar denoted by h.

- \u$x_1x_2x_3x_4$, where x_1--x_4 are hexadecimal digits, a shorthand for \u{$x_1x_2x_3x_4$}.

- \x$x_1x_2$, a shorthand for \u{x_1x_2}.

Otherwise \k is the same as k.

Dart strings also support *string interpolation*. String interpolation allows Dart expressions to be embedded within a string literal, as in:

```
print('The value of 2*2 is ${twice(2)}');
```

which prints The value of 2*2 is 4, assuming a reasonable implementation of twice() is in scope. As you can see, a $ sign indicates the appearance of an embedded expression, which is then delimited by curly braces. The embedded expression is evaluated and its toString() method called, and the result is inserted into the string at the point where the expression was given. If the expression consists of a single identifier, the curly braces may be elided:

```
var roomNumber = 101;
print('Welcome to room $roomNumber');
```

which prints Welcome to room 101.

In addition, Dart supports *raw strings*. Raw strings do not support escape sequences; they contain exactly what appears between the quotes. Raw strings come in both single line and multiline variants. Raw strings are prefixed with an r character.

```
print(r'A raw string \n'); // prints: A raw string \n, with no new line
```

Much like integers, string literals can be implemented by various classes, but this is undiscoverable except via reflection. Asking a string literal for its runtime type always yields String, which is the type the static checker ascribes to string literals as well. The class String cannot be subclassed or implemented by user code, just as with int, double, num and bool.

Dart represents strings as a sequence of UTF-16 code units. The Dart core library includes the Runes class that can convert a string into a unicode representation.

6.1.1.5 Symbols

Symbols are used to represent the names of declarations in a program. A symbol begins with a pound sign #, and is followed by either one or more dot-separated identifiers, or an operator. Here are some examples:

#MyClass #i #[] #com.evil_empire.forTheWin

Here are some illegal symbols:

#. #.. #++ #= #&= #|| #&&#!= #!

The above are all operators that are not user definable. The set of non-user-definable operators includes:[2]

- Assignment, including the basic assignment operator and all the compound ones
- Dots, as used in member selection, and double-dots, used in cascades
- Inequality, which is always defined in terms of the equality operator
- Negation via !
- Postfix operators: increment and decrement
- Logical Boolean operators

Naturally, the static type of a symbol literal is Symbol.

6.1.1.6 Lists

List literals are usually written as a comma-separated series of expressions delimited by square brackets.

All list literals implement the interface of class List. It is convenient to think of the literal [] is a shorthand for **new** List(), and ['a', 2, **true**] as a shorthand for:

```
new List() ..
        add('a')..
        add(2)..
        add(true);
```

Strictly speaking, the above interpretation is not true because the Dart implementation is not required to use the factory constructor of class List at all. However, as a first approximation, we are not far off.

---

2. To create symbols that do not have a literal form, one needs to explicitly invoke a constructor on class Symbol These situations typically arise in reflective code. Besides the operators listed above, there is the notable case of unary minus, whose name, for reflective purposes, is "unary-".

List is a generic class, and so one might reasonably ask whether [1, 2, 3] creates a List<int>? Does it correspond to:

```
new List() ..
        add(1)..
        add(2)..
        add(3);
```

or to:

```
new List<int>() ..
        add(1)..
        add(2)..
        add(3);
```

The answer (again, just as an approximation for pedagogical purposes) is the former. Dart does not try to infer a more precise type from the elements of the list literal. One reason is that performing such type inference at runtime is quite expensive. Another reason is optional typing.

To obtain the latter version, we can choose to provide a type argument explicitly by writing <int>[1,2,3]. In fact, the syntax $[e_1, \ldots, e_n]$ really is a shorthand for $<$ **dynamic** $> [e_1, \ldots, e_n]$. We can also think of the syntax $< T > [e_1, \ldots, e_n]$ as an approximation of:

```
new List<T>() ..
        add(e₁)..
        ...
        add(eₙ);
```

List literals can be made into compile-time constants as noted in Section 6.1.4 by prefixing them with the reserved word **const**. The use of **const** is orthogonal to the use type parameters. Hence **const**$[e_1, \ldots, e_n]$ is precisely a shorthand for **const** $<$ **dynamic** $> [e_1, \ldots, e_n]$, whereas **const** $< T > [e_1, \ldots, e_n]$ is a close approximation for:

```
const List<T>() ..
        add(e₁)..
        ...
        add(eₙ);
```

6.1.1.7 Maps

Map literals are written as a comma-separated series of key-value pairs delimited by curly braces. In each pair, the key is written first and separated from the value with a colon, that is, key: value.

All map literals implement the interface of class Map. It is convenient to think of the literal {} as a shorthand for **new** Map(), and of {'a': 'a', 'b': 2, 'c': **true**} as a shorthand for:

```
new Map() ..
    ['a'] = 'a'..
    ['b'] = 2..
    ['c'] = true;
```

As in the case of lists, the above interpretation is only an approximation because the Dart implementation is not required to use the factory constructor of class Map.

Map is a generic class with two type parameters—the first corresponding to the type of the keys, the second to the type of the values. The expression {'a':1, 'b': 2, 'c': 3} creates a Map<**dynamic, dynamic**> rather than a Map<String, int>.

We can choose to provide type arguments explicitly by writing <String, int>{'a':1, 'b': 2, 'c': 3}. In general, $\{ke_1 : ve_1, \ldots, ke_n : ve_n\}$ is a shorthand for $< \textbf{dynamic}, \textbf{dynamic} > \{ke_1 : ve_1, \ldots, ke_n : ve_n\}$. We can also think of the syntax $< K, V > [\{ke_1 : ve_1, \ldots, ke_n : ve_n\}$ as an approximation of

```
new Map<K, V>() ..
    [ke_1] = ve_1..
    ...
    [ke_n] = ve_n;
```

Map literals can be made into compile-time constants as noted in Section 6.1.4 by prefixing them with the reserved word **const**. The use of **const** is orthogonal to the use type parameters. Hence **const**$\{ke_1 : ve_1, \ldots, ke_n : ve_n\}$ is precisely a shorthand for **const** $< \textbf{dynamic}, \textbf{dynamic} > \{ke_1 : ve_1, \ldots, ke_n : ve_n\}$, whereas **const** $< K, V > \{ke_1 : ve_1, \ldots, ke_n : ve_n\}$ is a close approximation for:

```
const Map<K, V>() ..
    [ke_1] = ve_1..
    ...
    [ke_n] = ve_n;
```

6.1.1.8 Functions

Function literals were already discussed in Section 4.4. The rules for function types were given in Section 5.6. We can now give the type rules for function literals. There is no syntax for declaring an explicit return type for a function literal, so function literals always have return type **dynamic**. The argument types of a function literal are determined in the same way as any other function. If types are declared, they are used, otherwise the type of an argument is taken to be **dynamic**. Based upon the types of the arguments and whether they are required or optional, positional or named, the obvious function signature is determined. Examples:

```
(x) => 2*x; // (dynamic) → dynamic
(num a, num b){return a*b;} // (num, num) → dynamic
(String k, [Function f]) => m.putIfAbsent(k, f);
    // (String, [Function]) → dynamic
```

6.1.2   Identifiers

Identifiers in Dart are very similar to those in most other languages. An identifier can start with one of the characters A-Z, a-z, _ or $. Further characters can be any of the preceding or one of the numerals 0-9.

Dart does not allow non-ASCII letters in identifiers. This choice was made after much discussion. We chose to ensure that Dart programs be readable by virtually any professional programmer on earth, admittedly at the expense of convenience for users of non-Roman scripts.

An identifier, as its name suggests, identifies a declaration. It may identify a variable, a function or a type. An identifier might also denote a library, but then it cannot be used in an expression on its own.

When evaluating an identifier, the first step is to find the declaration it identifies. This involves a process of searching for the declaration, starting with the immediately surrounding scope. If no matching declaration (that is, a declaration whose simple name is the identifier we are searching for) is found, the search continues in the enclosing lexical scope, recursively, until the top level of the enclosing library. If we find a declaration, we have some idea what to do with it; but it may be that no declaration is found.

The search for the appropriate declaration is done statically by the compiler; once it knows what declaration is involved, it will generate the appropriate code to evaluate at runtime.

To see how this works, we'll look at the rather contrived code below:

```dart
var global = 0;
var shadowed = 1;

aFunction(x) => x*x + global + shadowed;

class AClass<T> {
  static var aClassVariable = 2;
  var anInstanceVariable = 3;
  static var shadowed = 4; // shadows top-level variable


  static aClassMethod() {
    print(shadowed);  // 4
    print(aClassVariable);  // 2
    print(anInstanceVariable); // error
  }


  aMethod(aParameter) {
    var aLocal = 5;
    var anUnassignedLocal;
    var shadowed = 6; // shadows static variable
    localFunction(x) => 7;
```

```
    {
      var moreLocal = 8;
      var shadowed = 9; // shadows local
      moreLocalFunction(y) {
        return moreLocal;
      }
      print(global); // 0
      print(shadowed); // 9
      print(aFunction);
      print(AnotherClass);
      print(F);
      print(AClass);
      print(T);
      print(aClassVariable); // 2
      print(anInstanceVariable); // 3
      print(aMethod);
      print(anotherMethod);
      print(aParameter);
      print(localFunction);
      print(aLocal); // 5
      print(anUnassignedLocal); // null
      print(moreLocal);  // 8
      print(moreLocalFunction);
    }
    print(shadowed); // 6
  }
  anotherMethod() => 10;
}

class AnotherClass{}

typedef int F(int x);
```

The simplest example is the evaluation of the identifier moreLocal. Our search finds a declaration of the same name in the immediately enclosing scope, which introduces a local variable. The identifier evaluates to the value stored in the local variable at the time of evaluation—in our case, 8. This is so obvious as to be painful, but it is necessary if one is to fully understand the rules. The situation with the identifier aLocal is almost exactly the same; the only difference is that we need to climb up the scope chain one more level to find the relevant declaration. And the case of anUnasssignedLocal is the same again, except that in the latter case the value of the expression will be null because the variable has not been initialized, whereas the former expression evaluates to 5.

Evaluating aParameter is very similar. The name aParameter is declared via a formal parameter declaration one more level up the scope chain, and the value of the formal parameter will of course vary from one invocation to the next.

What if the declaration we find does not denote a variable? There are several possibilities. The declaration might denote a function; the function might be a getter or a normal method (it cannot be a setter, because the name of a setter always ends with = and so is never an identifier).

If an identifier denotes a getter, the result of evaluation is the result of invoking the getter. If it is a static or top-level getter, we invoke it and return the result. If we have an instance getter, we invoke the getter on **this**.

As an example, consider the identifier shadowed. Inside aMethod it is first evaluated in the innermost scope, and so the innermost declaration is found, and the value of that variable, 9, is the result. At the very end of the method, we evaluate shadowed in the method's outermost scope, yielding a value of 6. Inside the class method aClassMethod, we reference shadowed again. Here, we begin in the method scope, and go up the scope chain until we reach the classes' static scope, which defines a getter for the class variable shadowed. Invoking this getter produces the value 4.

In contrast, inside the top-level function aFunction, shadowed evaluates to 1, because we start searching for a declaration inside the scope of aFunction, climbing upwards to the scope of its formal parameters and on to the library-level scope, where we find a suitable top-level getter implicitly declared. The same process works for global in that case; when we evaluate global inside of aMethod, our search will traverse a series of nested scopes until we reach the library scope.

If the declaration denoted by the identifier is for an instance method, then we extract a closure that will invoke the method on the current value of **this** when called, as described in Section 6.1.7.

Library methods, class methods and local functions are all treated the same; the result of evaluation is the function object (4.7) representing the function/method. For library or class methods, that object will be fixed; for local functions, a new object is created every time we enter the scope where the function is declared.

Another possibility is that id refers to a type declaration—either a class or a **typedef**. Every class and type alias is reified in Dart as a unique object, and that is the result of the evaluation in that case. However, the identifier could also denote a type variable. In that case, the result will be the value of the type variable at the time of evaluation—just like a normal variable. The type variable's value is a property of the receiver; any given instance of a generic class is constructed with actual type parameters via an instance creation expression like **new** List<String>. The actual type argument is itself an object tied to a type (String in this case) and that becomes the value of the corresponding formal type parameter.

Of course things can be more elaborate, as we saw in Chapter 5. For example, consider what happens when the identifier denotes a generic class such as List. No explicit value has been provided for List's type parameter. The default value for a type parameter is always **dynamic** so List denotes a type object representing class List<**dynamic**>.

Now suppose we don't find a declaration at all. That can happen in perfectly correct code; we might be referring to a member inherited from a superclass. The rule is that if we haven't found a declaration for id in the lexical scope, we evaluate id as if it was the expression **this**.id.

We can see this when we attempt to reference the instance variable anInstanceVariable inside of aClassMethod. However, this variable (and hence its getter) is not in scope. The reference is then interpreted as a getter call on **this**. In instance methods, this rule works well, allowing access to inherited members. Since accessing **this** inside a class method is illegal, this is a compile-time error in our case.

6.1.2.1   Reserved Words and Built-in Identifiers

Of course, identifiers cannot be reserved words. The following code will never parse correctly:

```
var if;
```

Not all of Dart's keywords are reserved words, however. Dart distinguishes *reserved words*, which may never be used to name entities in a Dart program, from *built-in identifiers*. Here are Dart's reserved words: **assert**, **break**, **case**, **catch**, **class**, **const**, **continue**, **default**, **do**, **else**, **enum**, **extends**, **false**, **final**, **finally**, **for**, **if**, **in**, **is**, **new**, **null**, **rethrow**, **return**, **super**, **switch**, **this**, **throw**, **true**, **try**, **var**, **void**, **while**, **with**. And here are the built-in identifiers: **abstract**, **as**, **deferred**, **dynamic**, **export**, **factory**, **get**, **implements**, **import**, **library**, **operator**, **part**, **set**, **static**, **typedef**.

Interesting situations arise with respect to Dart's built-in identifiers. Consider

```
get get => 'get'; // don't do this!
```

The above is perfectly legal, though very bad style. It defines a getter named get that returns the string 'get'. Get it? The Dart compiler can easily tell what each occurrence of "get" signifies, but since humans might not, this kind of code is strongly discouraged.

The distinction between reserved words and built-in identifiers allows for easier migration of code from other languages to Dart. In particular, it is often surprisingly easy to convert Javascript code to Dart. Allowing identifiers that would be legal in Javascript to be used in Dart, even when Dart has special uses for them, facilitates such migration.

Built-in identifiers may not be used as type names. Neither classes, typedefs nor type parameters may be given a name that is a built-in identifier. Built-in identifiers (except **dynamic**) cannot appear in type annotations either. This disallows situations like

```
get get get => new get(); // compile-time error
```

Obviously, you, the human reader, can immediate see that the intent is to define a getter named get that returns type get, but the parser would need to look several tokens ahead to make sense of what was going on. These restrictions do not impact migration since no types occur in Javascript programs. Furthermore, since types start with upper-case letters by convention, this rule poses no difficulty for Dart code. The only downside is to limit the employment opportunities for writers of puzzler books.

6.1.3   this

The reserved word **this**, used as an expression, refers to the receiver of the current method invocation. In addition, **this** can appear in the context of a constructor, where it denotes the newly created object. One cannot refer to **this** in a static or library method because no object was the receiver of the invocation.

Note that in a constructor, the keyword **this** can appear in the context of special formal parameters, and in redirecting constructors it marks calls to other constructors of the same class. However, neither of these uses of **this** are expressions in their own right.

6.1.4   Constants

A constant expression is an expression that may be evaluated at compile-time. The value of a constant expression can never change. Constants include literal numbers, Booleans, **null**, constant lists and maps, top-level functions, static methods as well as constant objects and a few specific compound expressions whose subparts are constants.

Constant objects are created by replacing **new** with **const** in instance creation expressions as shown in the next section. Constant object creation is only possible under very specific circumstances. The class must have a legal **const** constructor, and the arguments to the constructor must themselves be constants.

Given

```
library constants;

const aTopLevelConstant = 99;
thrice(x) => 3*x;

class Foo {
  static threeCubed() => thrice(thrice(3));
}

class Konst {
  final x;
  const Konst(this.x);
}
```

the following expressions are constants:

```
"def" 1 2.5 true false null const[7, 8, 9.0]   const{}
aTopLevelConstant thrice
Foo.threeCubed 'abc'  3+4
1 - 0 6*7 -1  2 > 3  3 <  3.0  7 >= 3+4
9 <= -0 17 % ( 2*2*2 + 8) '$aTopLevelConstant'
const Konst(42);
```

In contrast, these expressions are not constants:

```
thrice(2)
threeCubed == 0
'${const Point(0, 0)}'
const Konst(thrice(14));
```

6.1.5 Creating Objects

Objects are created by calling constructors, as described in Section 2.9. Constructors are called using *instance creation expressions*. The most common form of instance creation is **new** *ConstructorName*(*args*). Some examples:

```
new List<int>(); // calling a constructor with type arguments
new Map(); // calling a constructor of a generic class without type arguments
new Point.origin(); // calling a named constructor
```

Using **new** does not necessarily imply that a new instance is allocated. That depends on the constructor being called. The constructor might be a factory that obtains objects from a cache, directly or indirectly.

The other form of instance creation expression is

const *ConstructorName*(*args*)

which is used to create constant objects. In this case, the arguments to the constructors must all be constant objects or a compile-time error occurs.

Apart from **new** and **const**, the only way to call a constructor is either from within a constructor or via reflection (7). Within a constructor, super constructors are called either implicitly or via the forms **super**(*args*) or **super**.*id*(*args*). In addition, redirecting generative constructors can call other constructors using the syntax **this**(*args*) or **this**.*id*(*args*). Redirecting factories can name the constructor they will redirect to. The details of constructors are given in Section 2.9 as noted above.

6.1.6 Assignment

Assignments can be performed on top-level, class, instance and local variables. For top-level, class and instance variables, assignment is a sugar for invoking a setter.

For local variables, assignment acts the same way as in traditional languages, setting the value of the variable on the right-hand side of the assignment to be the result of evaluating the expression on the left-hand side.

One cannot assign to a final variable.

Assignments in Dart include simple assignments of the form variable = expression and compound assignments where the assignment is combined with an operator such as +. An example would be variable += expression, which is just sugar for variable = variable + expression. In addition to +=, we have -=, *=, /=, ~=, %=, <<=, >>= &=, ^=, |=.

As an example, the following program prints the numbers 1, -1, 303 and 10.

```
library another_lib;

var topLevelVariable = 101;

class SomeClass {
  static var classVariable = 100;
}


library my_lib;
import 'anotherLib.dart' as another show topLevelVariable, SomeClass;

var myTopLevelVariable = 0;

class MyClass {
  static var myClassVariable = 0;
}


main(){
  myTopLevelVariable += 1;
  MyClass.myClassVariable -= 1;
  another.topLevelVariable *= 3;
  another.SomeClass.classVariable /= 10;
  print(myTopLevelVariable);
  print(MyClass.myClassVariable);
  print(another.topLevelVariable);
  print(another.SomeClass.classVariable);
}
```

6.1.7 Extracting Properties

Occasionally it is convenient to use a method as an unevaluated function object. For example, we might want to register a method as a listener in an event loop. Assume that the function onClick() takes a listener function as an argument, eventually calling it back with an event object when a click event has occurred. Assume further that we have defined an instance method listener() to respond to click events.

```
listener(ev) => print(ev);
```

We can invoke onClick() as follows:

```
onClick(listener);
```

By the usual rules of the language, the above is a shorthand for

```
onClick(this.listener);
```

which in turn is (approximately) a shorthand for

    onClick((event) => **this**.listener(event));

In general, the notation $e.m$ denotes the method m of the object that e evaluates to. Strictly speaking, $e.m$ is a closure with exactly the same parameters as m. The effect of calling this closure with a given set of arguments is the same as invoking the method m on the value of e with those arguments. If m is in scope, one can use the identifier m instead of **this**.m.

Property extraction is actually a bit more than just a shorthand for writing a closure. The closures manufactured have a special implementation of equality as described in Section 4.7.

One cannot extract a getter or setter method in this fashion. With respect to getters, the issue is that if g is a getter, $e.g$ denotes the result of invoking the getter, and so that notation cannot be used to denote the getter method itself. As for setters, their true names end with = and are not proper identifiers, so $e.s$ = is not syntactically valid. In all such cases, one has to write a closure explicitly.

6.1.8 Method Access

Method access has the form $e.m(args)$, where e is an expression that produces an object, m is the name of a member, and $args$ is a possibly empty list of arguments. Examples:

    3.toString();
    {'a':1, 'b': 2}.containsKey('c');
    'abcd'.indexOf('cd', 1);
    myObject.foo(x, y, z);

It's important to understand the order in which things are evaluated. In member access, the receiver is computed first, then the arguments to the method. The arguments are, as for all function invocations, computed in left-to-right order. Usually this won't matter, but one can encounter situations where it makes a difference.

    String x;
    (x = 'xyz').indexOf(x); // evaluates to 0

If we did not compute the target expression (x = 'xyz') before computing the arguments, we would pass **null** as the argument. As a rule, if member access is sensitive to evaluation order, it is a sign of a problem in your code.

What if the method you are accessing does not exist? As you should well know by now, this will result in a call to noSuchMethod(). In fact, noSuchMethod() will get called if you call an existing method with the wrong number of arguments as well.

Another possible problem is that you are referring to a getter rather than a normal method. What actually happens in this case is that the expression $e.m(args)$ is interpreted as $(e.m)(args)$. First we perform a property access $e.m$, producing the result of calling the getter m. Next we invoke the **call** method on that result. If the result was a function object (or any other object that supports a suitable **call** method) then things will work as intended. Otherwise, we will get a noSuchMethod() again.

Using Operators

Operators in Dart are essentially instance methods with special syntax. A few of these are restricted so they may not be redefined in user code, but the majority are treated as ordinary instance methods that can be declared and/or overridden in any class.

The set of operators and their precedence is fixed. The following operators may be defined by user code: <, >, <=, >=, ==, -, +, /, ~/, %, ^, &, <<, >>, []=, [] and ~.

Most of these are binary operators. The exceptions are ~ which is unary, -, which comes in both unary and binary versions, and the indexed assignment operator, which is ternary. We have seen examples of user-defined operators before, starting with class Point. A similar example would be complex numbers:

```
class Complex {
  final num re, im;
  Complex(this.re, this.im);
  Complex.fromScalar(num s): this(s, 0);
  // nice example of redirecting constructor
  Complex operator + (Complex c) => new Complex(re + c.re, im + c.im);
  Complex operator * (Complex c) =>
  new Complex(re*c.re - im*c.im, re*c.im + im*c.re);
}
```

Operators are declared just like instance methods. The only difference is that the operator is written instead of an identifier as the method name, and the operator is prefaced with the keyword **operator**.

We've seen the indexing operators used on lists. We can now see that there is no special magic involved—any class can define indexing:

```
class Matrix {
  final List rows;
  Matrix.fromRows(this.rows); // assert all rows have same length
  Matrix.fromColumns(List cols);
  Matrix operator + (Matrix m) => new Matrix(pointwiseAdd(rows, m.rows));
  operator [](int index) => rows[index];
}
```

6.1.10 Throw

An expression of the form **throw** *e* throws an exception. The exception thrown is the result of evaluating the subexpression *e*. Unlike many other languages, **throw** is an expression, not a statement. This allows idioms such as:

```
unsupportedOperationFoo() => throw 'Foo is not supported, you imbecile!';
```

If **throw** were a statement, we could not use the shorthand syntax for functions and would have to write the more verbose:

```
unsupportedOperationFoo() {
  throw 'Foo is not supported, you imbecile!';
}
```

In general, expressions compose better than statements and it is advisable to define constructs as expressions rather than statements as often as possible.

As the examples show, any object can be thrown as an exception in Dart. There is no requirement that the object be an instance of a special exception class or a subclass thereof.

6.1.11 Conditionals

Conditional expressions have the form: $b\ ?\ e_1\ :\ e_2$ where b is a Boolean expression, and e_1 and e_2 are arbitrary expressions. If b evaluates to **true**, the overall value of the expression is the value of e_1; if b evaluates to **false** then the value of the conditional is the value of e_2.

What if b is not a Boolean value? In checked mode, the code will fail dynamically, as usual. In production, any non-Boolean value is treated as **false**. If the static type of b is not **bool** or **dynamic**, the type checker will warn you.

A conditional expression is another context where the fact that **throw** is an expression can be handy.

```
asExpected(x) ? computeNormalResult(x) : throw 'Unexpected input $x';
```

The type of a conditional is the least upper bound of the types of its two branches.

6.2 Statements

Here we discuss all of Dart's statements. They are for the most part what one would expect—the workhorses of programming such as **if**, **for**, **while** and so on. Technically, variable and function declarations are also statements, and almost any expression can be a statement as well.

6.2.1 Blocks

A *block* is a way of grouping several statements together. A block is delimited by curly braces in between which we may list statements. The list may be empty, like so {}. The statements within the block are separated by semicolons. Since blocks themselves are statements, blocks may nest.

The statements in a block are executed in sequence, left to right, top to bottom, in the order they appear in the source code.

Each block introduces its own scope. Declarations introduced within a block are only available inside the block. Within a block, you can refer to a declaration by its name, but only after the declaration. In other words, blocks do not allow mutually recursive declarations.

6.2.2   If

We've seen the **if** statement throughout the book. The reserved word **if** is followed by a parenthesized Boolean expression, followed by a statement, and optionally followed by an else clause consisting of the reserved word **else** and another statement. In both cases, the statement can be a simple statement:

```
if (x > 0) print(x);
if (y < x) print(y); else print(x);
```

or a block statement, which allows you to execute multiple statements in a single branch:

```
if (x > 0) { var y = 'in then branch'; print(x);};
```

Some people favor a style where one always uses block statements:

```
if (x > 0) {print(x);};
if (y < x) {print(y);} else {print(x);};
```

because one never needs to add/remove delimiters when adding statements to a branch or loop. Dart takes no position on the matter; it's up to you.

Dart gently encourages you to use proper Booleans in all tests, including **if** statements. You are likely to get a type warning if the expression you use in the condition is not a Boolean one; but only if we're really sure there's a problem.

For example, the code below:

```
String primeBeef(x) => isPrime(x) ? 'DEAD BEEF' : null;
if (primeBeef(23)) {print('Prime');} // warning
```

will generate a warning because strings are not Booleans. However, in the spirit of getting out of your way, in production mode Dart will not complain if your code is not typed, or if it is typed as Object:

```
primeBeef(x) => isPrime(x) ? 'DEAD BEEF' : null;
if (primeBeef(23)) {print('Prime');} // no complaints about truly dynamically typed code
```

The above will always fail in checked mode, however.

6.2.3   Loops

Dart supports several kinds of loops: **for** loops in two forms as well as **while** and **do** loops.

6.2.3.1   For Loops

Dart supports both the classical **for** loop syntax and a higher-level for-in syntax.

The latter is less error prone because it eliminates the risk of the off-by-one errors so common in C and other low-level languages. The for-in statement lets you perform a statement for a series of objects provided by an Iterable. An example of an Iterable might be a list:

```
import 'dart:math' show pow;
main() {
  var v;
  for (v in [1, 2, 4, 8]) print(pow(2, v)); // prints 2, 4, 16, 256
}
```

Here we iterate over a list and compute two to the power of each element in the list. We use the function pow imported from dart:math to compute the power. Each pass through the loop binds v to another element provided by the list.

It is possible to declare the iteration variable in the **for** statement itself, with or without a type declaration:

```
for (int v in [1, 2, 4, 8]) print(pow(2, v)); // prints 2, 4, 16, 256
for (var v in [1, 2, 4, 8]) print(pow(2, v)); // prints 2, 4, 16, 256
```

Besides lists, there are other classes that implement the Iterable interface. Most important, anyone can implement Iterable making instances of their class usable with the for-in statement.

The classic for loop has four parts: an initializer, a test, a loop variable update and the loop body. The initializer typically declares an iteration variable, but this is not strictly required. One can reuse an existing variable, though this is bad style. In any event, the initializer sets the initial value of the iteration variable. Then the loop evaluates the test; if the result is **true**, execution continues to the loop body. If the test expression is empty, it is taken to be **true** so that:

```
for (; ; ) s;
```

defines an infinite loop that executes s over and over. You can see that it is not strictly necessary to have an initializer or to define an iteration variable. On each iteration, after the loop body the loop update is executed and the test is repeated.

All of the above is totally standard and will come as no surprise to any trained programmer. However, there is one unusual twist to Dart's for loops.

Consider the following code, which allocates a list of 100 elements and sets each element to a closure. The closure is supposed to print the value of the iteration variable. After filling the list, we traverse it, list invoking each element in turn.

```
List<Function> funs = new List(100);
for (var index = 0; index < 100; index++) {
  funs[index] = () => print(index);
}
funs.forEach((f) => f());
```

In most languages the effect would be to print 99 a hundred times. Each of the closures would capture the same variable index, whose last value, set in the final iteration, was 99. This is perfectly logical, and yet many programmers are surprised by such behavior. In Dart, a fresh variable is allocated at each iteration and so the code above prints 0, 1, ..., 99.

6.2.3.2   While and Do

The most basic and most general of loops are **while** loops. A while loop evaluates
a condition, and if it holds it executes the loop body and then repeats the process
recursively; otherwise it terminates.

The **do** loop is a close cousin of **while**. It executes the loop body once, and then
evaluates a condition. If the condition holds, it repeats itself recursively, otherwise it
terminates.

The conditions evaluated by loops should yield a Boolean value. If the value is not
Boolean, it is taken to be **false**.

6.2.4   Try-Catch

To catch exceptions, one uses the **try** statement. A **try** statement consists of several
parts. The first part is a statement that might throw an exception. This is the statement
that immediately follows the **try** keyword. After that we might have one or more
catch clauses, a **finally** clause, or both. The **catch** clauses define handlers for specific
categories of exceptions. The **finally** clause defines cleanup code that is intended to be
executed no matter what happens—regardless of whether an exception has occurred or
not.

```
try {
  if ( x >= 0) {
    doSomething(x);
    } else { throw 'negative x = $x';}
}
on String catch(e) {
    print(s);
}
catch(o) { print('Unknown exception $o'); }
```

As noted earlier, one can throw any object, and consequently **catch** clauses can
catch any type of object as well. In the above example, we anticipate a string being
thrown. It is often convenient to throw a string that describes the problem encountered.
However, if the exception object is not a string, the second **catch** clause will come into
play, reporting the error. The second clause does not specify what type of object it
expects to catch, and so serves as a catch-all (no pun intended) for any exception that
might arise. The latter form of **catch** clause has the useful property of being compatible
with Javascript, easing the task of converting Javascript code into Dart.

The above behavior is quite standard. What makes **try-catch** different in Dart
is how stack traces are handled. Catch clauses optionally accept a second parameter
representing the stack trace. Only code that requires access to the trace should specify
the second parameter. If the parameter is not specified, the implementation may be
able to avoid filling in the stack trace. Filling in a stack trace is an expensive operation,
and avoiding it is an important optimization.

```
try {
  shootFloor();
}
on PodiatryException catch(e, s) {
  print(s);
  print('Shot myself in the foot: $e');
}
```

The stack trace object does not support any methods beyond those defined in Object. The most important among these is toString(), which prints out the stack trace.

6.2.5 Rethrow

It is not uncommon to catch an exception, and after examination decide that there is nothing to be done locally, and the exception should be propagated further up the call chain.

The **rethrow** statement deals with this exact situation by rethrowing an exception that is being processed in a **catch** clause.

6.2.6 Switch

The **switch** statement provides a way of choosing a course of action among a number of options based on the value of an expression. Each case handled by a switch corresponds to one possible value of the expression. The possible values must be known in advance— they have to be compile-time constants. We also insist that various cases be of the exact same type.

The best uses of **switch** are in applications like lexers or interpreters. Let's look at an absolutely trivial interpreter. The interpreter works on a very simple instruction set:

constant n
plus
minus

The instruction set assumes an implicit operand stack. The instruction **constant** n pushes the numeric constant n onto the stack; the **plus** instruction pops the two top elements of the operand stack, sums them and pushes the result back on the stack; **minus** is similar except that it subtracts rather than adds.

We can represent these instructions in various ways. Here is a very straightforward one:

```
class Instruction {
  String code;
  Instruction(this.code);
}
```

```
class LiteralInstruction extends Instruction {
  num constantValue;
  LiteralInstruction(this.constantValue): super('constant');
}
```

Now assuming that we have an iterable sequence of instructions instructions we can execute it using the following code:

```
List<num> operandStack = new List<num>();
for (Instruction instruction in instructions) {
  switch (instruction.code) {
    case 'plus':
        operandStack.add(operandStack.removeLast() + operandStack.removeLast());
      break;
    case 'minus':
        operandStack.add(operandStack.removeLast() - operandStack.removeLast());
      break;
    case 'constant':
      LiteralInstruction litInst = instruction;
      operandStack.add(litInst.constantValue);
      break;
  }
}
assert(operandStack.length == 1);
num result = operandStack.last;
```

We iterate over the instruction stream. On each iteration, the switch statement uses the op-code to direct processing as appropriate. Operands of the instructions are stored on a stack, operandStack. The stack is initially empty. A well-formed instruction stream should leave exactly one element on top of the stack when execution completes. That element is the result of evaluation.

While the above example is trivial and naive, it captures the essence of an interpreter. We can encode the instruction stream more efficiently (typically the instruction stream will be made up of integers, most likely bytes, rather than objects), and we are likely to have many more instructions, but the basic structure won't change much.

The workings of the switch statement in Dart are close to the traditional behavior in C and its successors, but not identical. In most languages, execution of a case "falls-through" to the next case. This decision, driven by implementation expediency decades ago, has been the source of countless bugs, in particular dangerous security bugs. In Dart, such falling-through is not allowed. If fall-through occurs, it will cause an immediate run time error, preventing hidden bugs. For this reason, each case in our example ends with a **break** statement, preventing fall-through.

One might naturally define the semantics such that execution simply terminates at the end of each case. This would be cleaner and simpler. However, we also want to make it easy to port code from other languages to Dart. The rules of Dart ensure that correctly written switch statements can be ported to Dart and are very likely to work as intended. Code that relies on fall-through will fail; such code is uncommon and error prone.

One can add a special default case to a switch statement. This case will be executed if none of the other cases match. We'll see an example below.

The switch statement has a number of requirements. The various cases must all be compile-time constants (2.11, 6.1.4). This allows for efficient compilation. Furthermore, the constants must either:

- All be instances of int, or

- All be instances of String, or

- All be instances of the exact same class and that class must inherit the implementation of == from Object.

If any of these requirements are violated, a compilation error will be flagged.

There is some subtlety to the above rules. Note that the requirement that all cases be of the same class is not imposed on integers. Dart implementations may use different classes to implement integers of widely varying size, yet the following is still allowed:

```
switch (guest.bankBalance) {
  case 0:
          print('Never darken my doorway again');
          break;
  case 10000000000:
          print('Welcome; su casa es mi casa');
          break;
  default: print('Hello');
  }
}
```

We only care that all the cases are of type int. Similar reasoning holds for type String, where again an implementation may use several classes depending on the nature of the strings used.

The ban on a user-defined equality method means that the implementation can quickly test whether an object matches a case using object identity (the default implementation of equality). This requirement is ignored for strings and integers; these have their own implementations of equality but it would not do to disallow the use of these types in switch statements.

6.2.7   Assert

Programmers live in a perpetual state of disappointment; their expectations are forever being dashed. Consider the humble factorial function:

```
factorial(int x) {
  return x == 0 ? 1 : x* factorial(x-1);
}
```

What could possibly go wrong with such simple code? In fact, sadistic software engineers are fond of asking this question in interviews. It is easy to be convinced of the correctness of the code above. It is also easy to evaluate factorial(-1); and see that the function will recurse until it runs out of stack space.

To guard against such heartbreak, it is good practice to make one's expectations explicit by generously sprinkling *assertions* in one's code. One makes such assertions by means of the **assert** statement.

Typically, one writes as assertion by enclosing a Boolean expression in an **assert**:

```
factorial(int x) {
  assert(x >= 0);
    return x == 0 ? 1 : x* factorial(x-1);
}
```

The above is very similar to:

```
factorial(int x) {
  if (x >= 0) return x == 0 ? 1 : x* factorial(x-1);
  else throw new AssertionError();
}
```

If the condition does not hold, an AssertionError is thrown. The advantage of the **assert** construct is that in production it is disabled, adding no overhead in space or time. It only has an effect in checked mode.

Of course, this might not be the best way to write factorial ; once we are clear about our assumptions, we probably want

```
factorial(int x) {
  if (x >= 0) return x == 0 ? 1 : x* factorial(x-1);
  else return 1;
}
```

or better yet:

```
factorial(int x) {
  if (x > 1) return x* factorial(x-1);
  else return 1;
}
```

The point is that one should think carefully about the assumptions one is making and then decide whether to validate them, and what to do if they do not hold.

It is also possible to provide a predicate inside the **assert**. In that case, the function will be called when the **assert** statement is executed. If it yields **true**, the assertion succeeds and all is well. Otherwise the assertion fails. This means that the assertion fails if the function returns **false** or if it returns any non-Boolean value.

The Dart type checker will complain if the expression within the **assert** is not one of the following types: bool, () → bool, or a type that is assignable to one of those. The only types assignable to bool are Object and **dynamic**. In the case of () → bool the possibilities are a bit more varied. Here are some assertions that won't cause warnings:

```
var x, y;
...
f() => false;
g() => x > y;
assert(f); // Fine, though will always fail in checked mode
assert(g); // Fine
assert(() => 'error!!'); // closures always have static return type dynamic
assert(([a, b]) => a > b ); // optional arguments are compatible
```

and here are some that will give rise to warnings:

```
String f() => 'true';
assert(f); // String return type incompatible with bool
assert((a, b) => a > b ); // incompatible arity
```

As noted in Chapter 5, checked mode treats type annotations as assertions. Every checked mode assignment of the form $T\ v = e$ is treated like the following production mode code:

$$T\ v = ()\ \{\textbf{var}\ \ v' = e;\ \textbf{assert}(\textbf{null} == v'\ ||\ v'\ \textbf{is}\ T);\ \textbf{return}\ v';\}();$$

Similar logic applies to parameter passing and to returning values from a function.

6.2.8 Return

The **return** statement transfers control from a function to its caller. There are two variants of **return**—one with an associated expression and one without:

```
return 42;
return;
```

The latter is essentially a shorthand for **return null**.

Executing a return statement will transfer control to the caller of the function immediately enclosing the **return**, at the point immediately following the call. The result of the current function is the value of the expression following the **return** (or **null**, if there is no expression). However, if the **return** is enclosed in a **try-finally** statement, control will transfer to the **finally** clause.

The Dart type checker will admonish us if the static type of the expression associated with the **return** cannot be assigned to the return type of the enclosing function. Furthermore, in checked mode, if the type of the value being returned is not a subtype of the declared return type, Dart will stop in its tracks (as always, **null** is ok).

The type checker will also warn if we write a **return** without an expression unless the surrounding function is declared to return type **dynamic** or **void**. So while the following is fine:

```
void postNotice(String n) {
   print(n);
   return;
}
```

as is:

```
postNotice(String n) {
   print(n);
   return;
}
```

this is not:

```
String postNotice(String n) {
   print(n);
   return;
}
```

In the last variant, we may have intended to return n to the sender, perhaps as part of a fluent API, which is why we declared the function to return String. Or we really never meant to return a string at all. In either case, something is not right, and Dart will issue a warning.

Return statements are treated specially in (generative) constructors. A **return** followed by an expression is disallowed in a generative constructor:

```
class Point {
   var x, y;
   Point(a, b) {return 0; } // ILLEGAL Dart:: compilation error!
}
```

Obviously, a constructor like Point() is supposed to return a new instance of Point and nothing else. That instance will be manufactured by the runtime and returned implicitly, so returning any other value makes no sense whatsoever.

In a generative constructor, we do allow a **return** without an accompanying expression, but we interpret it to mean **return this** rather than **return null**. In theory, we could also tolerate an explicit **return this** but no purpose is served by such a dispensation.

6.2.9   Yield and Yield-Each

Yield statements are used inside generator functions (4.8) to add new results to the collection being generated. A yield statement has the form **yield** e;.

A **yield** always causes its expression to be evaluated. Typically, the resulting value will be appended to the collection associated with the enclosing generator. If the generator is synchronous (4.8.2) then the associated collection is an iterable (4.8.1); if it is asynchronous (8.6.2), the associated collection is a stream (8.3).

Beyond this point the behavior of **yield** differs depending on whether the enclosing generator is synchronous or not. In the synchronous case, **yield** suspends the enclosing generator, and the call to moveNext() that caused the generator to execute will return to its caller with a value of **true**.

In the asynchronous case, execution of the generator continues.

Yield statements are only allowed inside generators.

The word **yield** is not a reserved word in Dart, nor even a built-in identifier. However, it is treated as a keyword inside a generator.

Sometimes, it is desirable to define a generator recursively.

```
naturalsDownFrom(n) sync* {
  if ( n > 0) {
    yield n;
    for (var i in naturalsDownFrom(n-1)) {
      yield i;
    }
  }
}
```

The code above is functionally correct, but a nasty performance bug lurks within: it runs in quadratic time. To see why, consider the following trace of naturalsDownFrom(3):

```
naturalsDownFrom(3)
→
  if ( 3 > 0) // true
    yield 3;
    for (var i in naturalsDownFrom(2))
    →
        if ( 2 > 0)
          yield 2;
          for (var i in naturalsDownFrom(1))
          →
              if ( 1 > 0)
                yield 1;
                for (var i in naturalsDownFrom(0))
                →
                    if ( 0 > 0) // false
                ← // returns the empty  sequence
              ← // the sequence 1
              yield 1;
        ← // the sequence  2, 1
        yield 2;
        yield 1;
← // the sequence 3, 2, 1
```

Notice that **yield** i; is executed $n-1$ times for the nth element in the sequence: once at each level of recursion; the first element, 3, is only yielded by the **yield** n; statement;

the second element, 2, is yielded once by **yield** n; and once by **yield** i;. The third element is 1, which is yielded once by **yield** n; and twice by **yield** i;.

Altogether we have $n(n-1)$ executions of **yield** i;, which is $O(n^2)$.

Dart provides the yield-each statement to address this problem. The yield-each statement has the form:

> **yield*** e;

The expression e must evaluate to a collection, or a runtime error will be raised; **yield*** appends all the elements of e to the collection associated with the enclosing generator.

We can rewrite our code using yield-each as follows:

```
naturalsDownFrom(n) sync* {
  if ( n > 0) {
    yield n;
    yield* naturalsDownFrom(n-1));
  }
}
```

The latter version runs in linear time.

6.2.10   Labels

Dart allows labels in code. The intent of labels is to facilitate automatic code generation by tools. We mention them here for the sake of completeness. However, you should never use labels in code you write. They are a low-level mechanism that should never appear in code that is written, or intended to be read, by humans.

6.2.11   Break and Continue

The statements **break** and **continue** support what might be called semi-structured control flow. They are a legacy of earlier languages in the C tradition. Typically they are useful when one is deep inside a control structure and needs to escape from the entire flow.

As an example, suppose we are processing messages in a loop. We keep processing messages until we get the message #stop. One way to handle this is to use an infinite loop and use **break** to escape from it.

```
var msg;
while (true) {
  msg = getMessage();
  if (msg == #stop) break; else processMsg(msg);
}
```

Another approach to the same problem is to test for the #stop message at the top of the loop:

```
var msg = getMessage();
while (msg != #stop) {
  processMsg(msg);
  msg = getMessage();
}
```

but this is perhaps less natural. However, one might do better to make the above a separate routine and use **return** to escape instead:

```
processMessages() {
  var msg;
  while (true) {
    msg = getMessage();
    if (msg == #stop) return; else processMsg(msg);
  }
}
```

Small methods are good programming style. A method has a name that helps documents the code's purpose, and moreover short methods are easier to read and comprehend than long ones with deeply nested control structures.

As a rule a **break** statement will escape from the nearest enclosing loop (be it a **while, do** or **for**) or **switch** statement. Any intervening **finally** clauses will be executed. If one writes a break statement that is not enclosed in a loop or **switch**, a compile-time error occurs.

One can also associate a **break** statement with a label. In that case, there must be an enclosing statement with the same label, and control will escape to that statement. Again, any intervening **finally** clauses will be executed. As noted in Section 6.2.10 above, labels (and **break** or **continue** statements that target them) should not be used in code written or read by humans. These constructs are there strictly to facilitate compilation into Dart.

The **continue** statement is very similar to **break** but is restricted to loops. Its effect is not to escape the loop, but to immediately continue to the next iteration.

6.3   Summary

Dart provides a fairly conventional spectrum of expressions and statements. The primary goal is to remain familiar to mainstream programmers. A few details vary, such as:

- The handling of Boolean items in conditionals and loops, motivated by Dart's aversion to runtime coercions.

- The rules for **switch**.

- The treatment of **for** loop variables, in order to prevent common errors.

- The handling of stack traces in **catch** clauses, driven by a desire to support more efficient exception handling.

- Allowing user-defined objects as constants.

- Operators, which are mostly treated as instance methods, as in, say, Smalltalk or Scala. Unlike those languages, the set of operators is restricted to a fixed set.

- Support for asynchrony.

Chapter 7

Reflection

What is reflection? For our purposes, reflection is the ability of a program to examine or modify itself. Reflection can be further subdivided into *introspection*, the ability of a program to determine its structure while running, and *self-modification*, its ability to change itself while running.

At this time, Dart only supports introspection. We expect support for self-modification to evolve over time.

Reflection in Dart is based on the concept of *mirrors*. A *mirror*, in this context, is an object that reflects another object. Mirrors are a particular form of reflective APIs that have advantages with respect to distribution, deployment and security, which we will discuss in depth in Section 7.2. First, we'll build up an understanding of why and how we might use mirrors.

7.1 Introspection

In Dart, one may introspect on libraries, classes and functions, as well as objects. If you wish to reflect on an entity in Dart, you need to obtain a mirror on it. There are mirrors corresponding to the various entities that one may reflect upon: library mirrors, class mirrors, method mirrors, object mirrors and so on. In all these cases, the first step is to import the mirror library provided by the Dart platform:

```
import 'dart:mirrors';
```

As usual, good style will dictate that we explicitly specify what members of **dart:mirrors** we intend to use. As an example, let's write some code to reflectively print out the members of a class:

```
import 'dart:mirrors' show reflectClass, ClassMirror;


class SuperClass {
  int superField = 0;
  final int superFinalField = 1;
  int get superGetter => 2;
  set superSetter(x) {}
  int superMethod(x) => 4;
```

```
  static int superStaticField = 5;
  static final int superStaticFinalField = 6;
  static const int superStaticConstField = 7;
  static int get superStaticGetter => 8;
  static set superStaticSetter(x) {}
  static int superStaticMethod(x) => 10;
}


class SelfPrinting extends SuperClass {
  int aField = 11;
  final int aFinalField = 12;
  get aGetter => 13;
  set aSetter(x) {}
  int aMethod(x) => 15;
  static int staticField = 16;
  static final int staticFinalField = 17;
  static const int staticConstField = 18;
  static int get staticGetter => 19;
  static set staticSetter(x) {}
  static int staticMethod(x) => 20;
}


main() {
  ClassMirror cm = reflectClass(SelfPrinting);
  for (Symbol memberName in cm.instanceMembers.keys) {
    print('$memberName');
  }
}
```

The application uses the top-level function reflectClass() defined in dart:mirrors to obtain a mirror on the class SelfPrinting. The result is an instance of ClassMirror that supports the getter method instanceMembers. Invoking instanceMembers on a class mirror returns a map, keyed by the names of the instance members of the reflected class. The map's keys constitute a list of the names of the class' instance members, which we can print directly.

Running this application should print[1]

```
Symbol("==")
Symbol("hashCode")
Symbol("toString")
Symbol("noSuchMethod")
```

---

1. If you run this and see printouts of the form Symbol("gobbledygook"), make sure you disable minification, which is described in Section 7.1.1 below.

```
Symbol( "runtimeType" )
Symbol( "superField" )
Symbol( "superField=" )
Symbol( "superFinalField" )
Symbol( "superGetter" )
Symbol( "superSetter=" )
Symbol( "superMethod" )
Symbol( "aField" )
Symbol( "aField=" )
Symbol( "aFinalField" )
Symbol( "aGetter" )
Symbol( "aSetter=" )
Symbol( "aMethod" )
```

The printed values are all instances of class Symbol, which are used to represent the names of reflected entities throughout the Dart mirror API. We'll have more to say about symbols in the next section.

A few things to notice about the list above. For the fields superField and aField, two entries are listed. One is a getter, and the other (ending with =) is a setter. The instanceMembers method is designed to provide us with the API of an instance—the set of members one can invoke. Since fields are never accessed directly in Dart, the results do not actually include a mirror on a field declaration. Instead, mirrors on the implicitly defined getter and setter methods are provided. That is why the final fields only show up once in the list: final fields give rise to getters but not to setters.

The list includes the inherited members as well as those declared by SelfPrinting itself. These include the members of Superclass and of Object. Again, what instanceMembers gives us is the API an instance of class SelfPrinting and that includes inherited members.

Since we asked for the instance members, the static members are not listed, nor are the constructors. This makes sense, because neither may be invoked via instances of the class. Suppose we change our for loop slightly:

```
for (Symbol memberName in cm.staticMembers.keys) {
    print('$memberName');
}
```

Now we get   Symbol("staticField")

```
Symbol( "staticField=" )
Symbol( "staticFinalField" )
Symbol( "staticConstField" )
Symbol( "staticGetter" )
Symbol( "staticSetter=" )
Symbol( "staticMethod" )
```

Once again, see how the both getters and setters for mutable fields like staticField are listed. The static members of SuperClass do not appear in this list; static members are not inherited and cannot be invoked via SelfPrinting.

7.1.1   Implications for Speed and Size

If you are running your code directly on a Dart virtual machine, you can assume that the entire Dart platform, as well as your complete application source, are available at runtime. However, there are many deployment scenarios where this is not the case.

The most common of these is when you compile Dart into Javascript for deployment to web browsers. Dart-to-Javascript compilers seek to minimize the size of the code they generate. The smaller the generated code, the faster the download over the network, and the less time is occupied parsing the source code at program startup. The process of minimizing deployed code size interacts with reflection in a number of ways, however.

7.1.1.1   Tree Shaking

Compilers will avoid generating code that is never used. Using a process known as *tree shaking*, the compiler determines whether certain code is actually used in a given application. If an application uses only a single function from a large library, there is no need to generate, download and parse all the other code in that library. In fact, it is critical to avoid doing so; imagine if every web page using Dart had to download the code for the entire set of Dart core libraries. Even a simple "Hello World" program would be several megabytes in size!

Reflection presents a difficulty. It is very hard to predict what code is being invoked reflectively. An implementation might choose to be conservative and assume that if reflection is used, all code in the system must be preserved in the generated output since it might be invoked reflectively. The result would be that any use of reflection would carry a major penalty in code size, with adverse implications for startup time and memory footprint. At the other extreme, an implementation could decide to ignore the use of reflection when tree shaking. The unfortunate consequence would be that reflective calls that worked during testing and development might fail in production because the code they needed was not there.

In practice, current implementations take the former approach. However, the problem can be managed using metadata annotations and the **reflectable** package, as described in Section 7.4.

7.1.1.2   Minification

The term *minification* refers to the process of compacting symbols in a source program being downloaded to a web browser. Names used in the source code are mangled into shorter names used in the compiled code. The program that performs minification is called a *minifier*.

The minifier does not act on string literals; these typically represent user data that needs to be preserved; a string may be printed for human consumption, or used as a key in an external database, and so it cannot safely be mangled.

Minification has unfortunate consequences for reflection. It is natural to use strings to represent the names of declarations. However, once a program has been minified, these strings no longer correspond to the actual names of entities in the program.

To mitigate the damage caused by minification, Dart reflection uses symbols[2] (6.1.1.5) rather than strings as keys. Symbols are recognized by the minifier and are transformed using the same mangling used for identifiers in the code.

At times it may be necessary to map between symbols and human-readable strings. We might want the self-printing code in the previous section to print out the names of the members directly, rather than in the form Symbol(...). This is even more crucial in the presence of minification; a minified program will print out symbols with minified names, which is not likely to be useful to a human reader. To avoid such problems, the mirror API supports conversion between symbols and human-readable strings in both directions. The class MirrorSystem includes the methods:

```
static String getName(Symbol symbol);
static Symbol getSymbol(String name, [LibraryMirror library])
```

To convert a symbol into a string representing its unminified name, use getName. The inverse operation is getSymbol; it will produce a symbol based on a human-readable string.

We can use this functionality to refine our self-printing example. We add MirrorSystem to the **show** clause of our import, and call MirrorSystem.getName() to do the necessary conversion.

```
import 'dart:mirrors' show ClassMirror, MirrorSystem, reflectClass;


class SuperClass {
// unchanged from above
}


class SelfPrinting extends SuperClass {
// also unchanged
}


main() {
  ClassMirror cm = reflectClass(SelfPrinting);
  for (Symbol memberName in cm.instanceMembers.keys) {
    print('${MirrorSystem.getName(memberName)}');
  }
}
```

Running the code above prints

```
==
hashCode
```

---

2. Indeed, reflection was the main motivation for adding symbol literals to Dart.

```
toString
noSuchMethod
runtimeType
superField
superField=
superFinalField
superGetter
superSetter=
superMethod
aField
aField=
aFinalField
aGetter
aSetter=
aMethod
```

irrespective of minification. Self-printing code is not necessarily the most popular application, however. Having established the basics, we will now consider somewhat more realistic uses of reflection.

7.1.2   Example: Proxies

In Section 2.10 we defined a general-purpose proxy class Proxy. It's implementation relied on a helper method runMethod(). We are finally in a position to show the implementation of runMethod():

```
runMethod(forwardee, Invocation inv){
    InstanceMirror im = reflect(forwardee);
    im.delegate(inv);
}
```

The first step is to obtain a mirror on forwardee using the top-level function reflect() from dart:mirrors. Instances are mirrored by class InstanceMirror. Instance mirrors support the method delegate(), which takes an Invocation and executes the corresponding method on the reflected object with the arguments given by the invocation.

In reality, we'd like to avoid allocating an instance mirror on every call. We'll rewrite Proxy so that we cache the instance mirror in a private instance variable.

```
library proxies;

import 'dart:mirrors' show InstanceMirror, reflect;

@proxy class Proxy {
    InstanceMirror _im;
    get forwardee => _im.reflectee;
```

```
Proxy(f){
    _im = reflect(f);
}
noSuchMethod(inv) => _im.delegate(inv);
}
```

To maintain the original interface, we define a getter for the forwardee. Most mirrors have an accessor named **reflectee** that returns the entity the mirror reflects; here we use **reflectee** to implement **forwardee**. The completed class carries the **@proxy** annotation described in Section 5.7.6 to reduce unnecessary warnings.

7.1.3   Example: Serialization

We speak of *object serialization* when we mean to write an object to an external medium. Likewise, *object deserialization* refers to reading an object from an external medium. The external medium could be persistent storage, or it could be a communications channel. Serializing objects is useful if we want to save program state persistently, or if we are communicating with a remote process at the level of objects. We shall see examples of the latter in Chapter 8.

The topic of object serialization is a rich one, and we will not confront it in its full glory here. The serializer/deserializer we show here is necessarily simplistic; it is neither robust nor complete nor performant. There are different approaches to serializing objects with advantages and disadvantages that we will not discuss. Despite these many caveats, we choose serialization as an illustrative example because it is a classic application of reflection.

A serializer needs to define a standard representation for objects. We will represent an object via its class and fields. Specifically, we'll store the name of the class, the name of the library in which it was defined, and the contents of the fields of the object.

Suppose we wish to serialize an object s_o created via the expression **new** Point(42, 91). Recall that Point was defined within library **points** in Section 1.4. The serialized form of s_o would be points/Point(42 91).

What if we had code like:

```
var shared = new Point(42, 91);
var so = new Pair(shared, shared);
```

where Pair is the class declared in Section 2.7. The proposed format is no longer adequate. Assuming Pair is declared in library **pairs**, the serialized form would be

pairs/Pair(points/Point(42 91) points/Point(42 91))

but that does not capture the structure correctly. The Pair object ends up referencing two distinct instances of Point rather than the single Point object **shared**. The problem is that source programs are always trees, but objects can form directed graphs. We must generalize our representation to support such graphs.

To support sharing, we will use integer indices to represent references to objects. The representation of an object is then the fully qualified name of the class, followed by the actual parameter list, where parameters are represented via integer indices. The serialized form of **new** Pair(shared, shared) would be pairs/Pair(1 1).

The complete serialized form of an object graph would be a list of such serialized objects. Integer indices would refer to elements of the list. In our example the graph could be written [pairs/Pair(1 1), points/Point(2 3), 42, 91]. The Pair object itself is at index 0, the shared instance of Point is at index 1, the integer 42 is at index 2 and the integer 91 is at index 3.

All this leads us to the following definition:

```
class SerializedObject {
  final int id;
  final Symbol libName;
  final Symbol className;
  List<int> fields;
  SerializedObject(this.id, this.libName, this.className);
  toString(){
    String args = (fields.map((a) => a.toString())).fold('', (s, e) => '$s $e');
    return '${MirrorSystem.getName(libName)}/${MirrorSystem.getName(className)}($args)';
  }
}
```

A serialized object has a unique integer identifier id and records the name of its class and enclosing library, as well as the contents of its fields. These fields are represented as the integer IDs of the objects they contain.

The toString() method uses this information to produce the serialized form of an object.

There are several classes of common Dart objects provided by the system, whose representation is opaque. These include literals such as **null**, numbers, Booleans, strings and symbols. We'll use a specialized representation for these:

```
class SerializedLiteral implements SerializedObject {
  final int id;
  final literal;
  SerializedLiteral(this.id, this.literal);
  Symbol get className => #literal;
  Symbol get libName => #literal;
  List<int> get fields => [];
  set fields(f){}
  String toString() => literal is String ? '"$literal"' : literal.toString();
}
```

The class SerializedLiteral emulates the SerializedObject interface. In fact, many of the emulated members are never used, and are defined only to formally comply with the required interface. We could have chosen not to implement these and ignore the resulting warnings. Or we could have defined a common superinterface for SerializedLiteral and SerializedObject, which would require us to be more discriminating in the deserialization code to come (or ignore warnings there, too).

Lists and maps also have special syntax and representations in Dart. They are more involved than the literals mentioned above because they reference other objects. We'll only deal with lists here, to keep things simple. The extension to maps is left as an exercise to the reader.

```
class SerializedList implements SerializedObject {
  final int id;
  List<int> fields;
  SerializedList(this.id, List l){fields = l.map((e) => serializeObject(e).id).toList();}
  Symbol get className => #List;
  Symbol get libName => #literal;
  String toString() {
    StringBuffer buffer = new StringBuffer();
    buffer.writeAll(['[']);
    for (int f in fields) {buffer.writeAll([f, ' ']);}
    buffer.writeAll([']']);
    return buffer.toString();
  }
}
```

Like all serialized objects, a serialized list requires an integer id. The serialized form of lists retains the contents of the list as a list of indices. The toString() method gives the serialized form of a list as list of indices bounded by square brackets. And as before, we make sure we emulate the rest of the SerializedObject interface.

7.1.3.1 The Serialization Algorithm

We can now proceed to write our serializer.

```
library serializer;

import 'dart:mirrors' show
            ClassMirror, InstanceMirror, MethodMirror, Mirror, MirrorSystem,
            reflect, VariableMirror;


Map<Object, SerializedObject> sos;
// the serialized objects
int counter;
```

As we serialize the object graph, we will store its serialized form into a map sos, keyed by the object itself. Each time we serialize an object, we assign it an integer index. That index is the current value of counter. We increment counter after each object is serialized.

We need to detect cycles in the object graph to prevent an infinite loop while serializing. We'll see exactly how this works shortly.

We also need a couple of utility functions. The isLiteral function identifies objects of known types that we handle specially.

```
bool isLiteral(o) {
  return o is num || o is bool || o is String  || o is Symbol || null == o;
}
```

The function superclasses computes all the superclasses of a given class. It is a useful convenience often needed when processing class hierarchies reflectively. It isn't part of dart:mirrors, however, because we want to keep the core of Dart small.

```
List<ClassMirror> superclasses(ClassMirror cm) {
  List<ClassMirror> scs = new List<ClassMirror>();
  ClassMirror scm = cm;
  while (scm != null) {
    scs.add(scm);
    scm = scm.superclass;
  }
  return scs;
}
```

The logic of the function is straightforward; it relies on the method superclass of ClassMirror that returns (a class mirror on) the superclass of the class reflected by the mirror. For Object, the result of superclass is **null**. All we have to do is go up the superclass chain and add the classes to our result list. Here we consider the superclass relation to be reflexive, so the superclass list of a class contains the class itself. This formulation turns out to be convenient in the code below.

Now we can focus on the serialization algorithm proper. The entry point is the function serialize, which takes the root of an object graph and serializes the graph.

```
List <String> serialize(o) {
  counter = 0;
  sos = new Map<Object, SerializedObject>();
  serializeObject(o);
  List <String> sf = new List<String>(sos.values.length);
  for (var v in sos.values) {sf[v.id] = v.toString();}
  return sf;
}
```

All serialize does is initialize counter and sos, call serializeObject on the root and package the results in a list, in the order of the serialized object IDs. Most of the work is done by the serializeObject routine, which serializes an object and its fields recursively.

```
SerializedObject serializeObject(o){
  SerializedObject current = sos[o];
  if (current != null) {
    return current;
  }
  if (isLiteral(o)) {return sos[o] = new SerializedLiteral(counter++, o);}
```

```
    if (o is List) {
      return sos[o] = serializeList(o);
    }
    InstanceMirror im = reflect(o);
    ClassMirror cm = im.type;
    var res = sos[o] = new SerializedObject(counter++, cm.owner.simpleName, cm.simpleName);
    res.fields = serializeFields(cm, im);
    return res;
  }
```

We begin by looking up the object in the serialized object map sos. If we find it, that means we have already encountered it and can return its serialized form. This ensures we represent sharing correctly and prevents us from going into an infinite recursion on cyclic object graphs.

Assuming we haven't encountered o before, we check whether it is a literal; if so, we produce a suitable SerializedLiteral, store it in sos and return it. Likewise, we check whether the object is a list, and if so create a SerializedList using the following routine:

```
SerializedList serializeList(List l) {
  SerializedList sl = new SerializedList(counter++);
  sl.fields = l.map((e) => serializeObject(e).id).toList();
  return sl;
}
```

Otherwise, we have an ordinary object o to serialize. We get a mirror on o and then obtain a mirror on its class. We can obtain a mirror on an object's class via its instance mirror, using the type() method. Unlike runtimeType, type returns us a mirror on the true class of the underlying object.

The ClassMirror provides with the name of the class using the method simpleName(). We can also get a mirror on its containing library using the method owner. The owner method returns a mirror on the enclosing declaration of the entity being reflected. In the case of a class, the owner is always a library. For methods and functions, the owner might be a library or a class or another function. The point is that one can traverse the lexical scope of a declaration using owner.

In our case, all we want is the name of the enclosing library, which we can compute using owner.simpleName(). We could have obtained the fully qualified name of the class directly using qualifiedName() but we prefer to obtain and store the names separately. As we'll see later, it will make things a bit easier during deserialization.

We can then allocate an instance of SerializedObject, using the value of counter as its ID. We increment counter so that it's ready for the next object, and store the new SerializedObject in sos. We then call serializeFields, which produces a list of indices for the fields of the object, set the fields of the serialized object accordingly, and return.

All that remains is to show how serializeFields works. We iterate through the superclasses using our handy utility function, and for each superclass, iterate through the members it declares, selecting only the instance field declarations. For each such field, we extract its value reflectively using the getField method on instance mirrors. This returns a mirror whose reflectee is the object stored in the field. We serialize said object and add its ID to the list of results.

```
List<int> serializeFields(ClassMirror cm, InstanceMirror im) {
  List<int> fields = new List<int>();
  for (ClassMirror sc in superclasses(cm)) {
    for (Mirror m in sc.declarations.values.where(isInstanceField)) {
      fields.add(serializeObject(im.getField(m.simpleName).reflectee).id);
    }
  }
  return fields;
}
```

Note that we use the method declarations rather than instanceMembers. Whereas instanceMembers would provide us with the interface an instance of the mirrored class supports, declarations provides us with a list of the members declared by the class itself (as opposed to anything that is inherited). And while instanceMembers always consists of mirrors on methods (be they getters, setters or ordinary methods), declarations includes the members actually declared: fields and constructors as well as methods. A getter or setter method will appear in declarations only if it was explicitly declared by the programmer, whereas instanceMembers will include the implicitly generated getters and setters for a field rather than the field itself.

For our current purposes, we want to gather the actual fields of the class, as they define the object graph rooted at the object. Once we have all the relevant declarations, we select those declarations that are instance variables using isInstanceField, a simple convenience function shown below.

```
bool isInstanceField(Mirror m) => m is VariableMirror && !m.isStatic;
```

A field is always reflected by a VariableMirror, and no other kind of member will be reflected by a variable mirror. Thus, we can test whether a given declaration is a field by testing the type of the mirror. Variable mirrors support a variety of accessors that allow us to query the properties of the underlying variable declaration. Here we use isStatic to ensure we are dealing with an instance variable.

There is a flaw in the approach we have outlined. For historical reasons get-Field(fieldName) actually invokes the getter named fieldName rather than accessing the field directly. As a consequence, if a field is hidden by another field of the same name, or has its getter overridden, things will go wrong. We expect to correct this situation in the mirror library in the near future.

See https://github.com/google/serialization.dart for an example of a much more serious tool for serialization. Our goal here is to illustrate the use of reflection, not to show how to write a serializer.

7.1.3.2   Deserialization

The deserializer brings up additional issues.

```
library deserializer;

import 'serializer.dart' as serializer show isInstanceField, SerializedList,
                                    SerializedLiteral, SerializedObject;
import 'dart:mirrors' show ClassMirror, currentMirrorSystem, InstanceMirror,
                    LibraryMirror, MethodMirror, Mirror,  MirrorSystem,
                    VariableMirror;
import 'dart:math' as math show pow;
import '../grammars/CombinatorialParsing.dart' show CombinatorialParser,
                                    ExecutableGrammar, Token;


Map<int, dynamic> dsos; // the deserialized objects
List<String> serializedForm;
CombinatorialParser parser = new SerializedObjectParser().serializedObject;
int sid;
```

We keep the objects we deserialize in a map, dsos, keyed by their index in the
serialized form. The map is initially empty. The deserializer simply iterates over the
serialized form produced by the serializer, which is just a list of strings. We deserialize
each element of the list in turn, using the function deserializeString:

```
deserialize(List<String> sf) {
  sid = 0;
  dsos = {};
  serializedForm = sf;
  // serialized form is a list of strings. Go thru each in turn and
  // deserialize
  for(String s in sf) {
    deserializeString(s);
    sid++;
  }
  return dsos;
}


void deserializeString(String s) {
  if (dsos[sid] == null) {
    deserializeObject(parser.parse(s));
  }
}
```

In turn, deserializeString parses the serialized form of a single object into a SerializedObject. It checks to see whether the current object ID has already been parsed, to deal

correctly with sharing and cycles. It then parses the serialized form and passes that to deserializeObject. The code relies on the function parse. In the next section, we will describe a framework that makes it easy to construct parsers. We will then define parse using that framework. In the meantime, you'll have to believe that parse does its job.

Ideally, we'd like to avoid running any user code, such as a constructor, during deserialization. However, we need some way of creating the object we are deserializing. In some systems, there is a mechanism to allocate a raw instance of a class without executing a constructor. For example, in languages of the Smalltalk family, classes support a method basicNew, and on the JVM, the new bytecode acts in a similar way. At the time of this writing, Dart does not expose such functionality.

Using basicNew or its equivalent, one can produce an instance in an improperly initialized state. This is problematic, as it can lead to security problems. So one really has to be very careful how such functionality is exposed. Nevertheless, we believe that this could be exposed via suitably structured mirrors, especially since Dart mirrors play no security role.

Given a raw instance, one could then use reflection to set all its fields based on the serialized object description, producing an exact deserialization of the original.

How do we create a raw instance in the absence of basicNew? We are going to play a rather dirty trick. We will call a constructor, but we will feed it special proxy objects as arguments. These objects respond to all method invocations by returning themselves.

```
@proxy class OmniProxy {
  noSuchMethod(Invocation) => this;
}
```

Instances of OmniProxy will service all method invocations the constructor invokes upon them, directly or indirectly. Of course the resulting object is in a completely incoherent state, but that would also be true of the raw object we would have gotten from basicNew. Once we have the raw object in hand, we will set its state correctly using reflection.

We can now examine how to deserialize a single SerializedObject. We look up the library to which the serialized object's class belongs, and then look up the class within that library. We then choose a constructor for the class. We don't really care which constructor it is, so we pick the first one we find. We use the constructor to create an instance of the class, passing instances of OmniProxy as arguments.

All of this is accomplished by the code below:

```
OmniProxy filler = new OmniProxy();

deserializeObject(serializer.SerializedObject so) {
  if (so is serializer.SerializedLiteral) {
    return dsos[so.id] = so.literal;
  }
  if (so is serializer.SerializedList) {
    return deserializeList(so);
  }
```

```
// Find the library for the object's class; assume library exists in
// current isolate
LibraryMirror lib = currentMirrorSystem().findLibrary(so.libName);
// get hold of the class, and get a mirror on it
ClassMirror cm = lib.declarations[so.className];
MethodMirror constructor = cm.declarations.values.firstWhere(
      (d) => (d is MethodMirror) && (d.isConstructor)
);
List cargs = [];
for (int i = 0; i < constructor.parameters.length; i++) {
  cargs.add(filler);
}
InstanceMirror im = cm.newInstance(constructor.constructorName, cargs);
// invoke the constructor
dsos[so.id] = im.reflectee;
Iterable fields = so.fields.map((int f) => deserializeIndex(f));
//deserialize the fields
setFields(im, cm, fields);
return im.reflectee;
}
```

We use currentMirrorSystem to find the library in which the object originated. We assume the correct library exists in the current isolate; more robust code would check the result and throw an exception if this assumption was invalid. We now have a LibraryMirror whose declarations include all top-level library members. We then look up the class named in the serialized form in the declarations, yielding a ClassMirror. We can then search its declarations for a constructor. We first filter out everything that isn't a MethodMirror. Once we know we are dealing with a method mirror, we can safely ask whether it is a constructor using the isConstructor getter, which is only defined on method mirrors. We can then ask the class to create an instance using the constructor. We pass an appropriate number of proxies as arguments. The result is an instance mirror. We store the mirror's reflectee, which is the deserialized object, in dsos, at the index of the serialized object.

As discussed above, the deserialized object is in an incorrect state, computed based on proxies. We now deserialize the fields. The fields are given by indices in the serialized object, and we obtain the deserialized object corresponding to each such field by passing the index to deserializeIndex(). Finally we set the deserialized object's fields to the correct values using setFields() and return the result.

The function deserializeIndex() looks up the serialized form based on index and then uses deserializeString() to deserialize it. The manipulation of sid is necessary to allow deserializeString() to check whether the object has already been deserialized; lastly, the deserialized object is returned.

```
deserializeIndex(int index){
  int oldId = sid;
  sid = index;
```

```
  deserializeString(serializedForm[index]);
  sid = oldId;
  return dsos[index];
}
```

Deserializing a list is a special case, but quite similar to deserializing a regular object.

```
deserializeList(serializer.SerializedList sl){
  List res = new List(sl.fields.length);
  dsos[sl.id] = res;
  Iterable elems = sl.fields.map((e) => deserializeIndex(e));
  int i = 0;
  for (var e in elems) {res[i++] = e;}
  return res;
}
```

For completeness, here is the code for setFields():

```
int setFields(InstanceMirror im, ClassMirror cm, Iterable fields) {
  int fieldIndex = 0;
  // iterate over all fields, including superclasses
  if (cm.superclass.reflectedType != Object) {
    fieldIndex = setFields(im, cm.superclass, fields);
  }
  for (VariableMirror vm in cm.declarations.values.where(serializer.isInstanceField) {
    im.setField(vm.simpleName, fields.elementAt(fieldIndex++));
  }
  return fieldIndex;
}
```

The setFields() method fills in fields of an object specified via an instance mirror im. The class mirror cm specifies which fields should be filled in; only those fields declared by the class represented via cm and its superclasses are filled in. The fields themselves are specified via an iterable fields. The code recurses up the class chain until it reaches a direct subclass of Object. Object is known to not have any fields so there is no point visiting it. For each class visited, we loop through the instance variables reflectively and use the method setField to set each field in turn. We keep track of the fields processed using fieldIndex.

This approach we have outlined is inherently limited. Like all general-purpose proxy schemes in Dart, it will not work correctly in the presence of type tests and casts, or in checked mode. It will not work well if constructors rely on side effects (which they should not). In some odd situations, constructors relying on identity (or lack thereof) between arguments might have difficulty as well. The same is true if the constructor relies on any operator that cannot be redefined.

Irrespective of the use of proxies, setting fields via reflection is problematic, because setField actually invokes a setter method, which could be overridden or hidden. This is similar to the issue with getField discussed earlier. Ultimately Dart should support a reflective operation that actually modifies a specific instance variable. Again, our purpose here is pedagogical, and so we have set all these reservations aside.

7.1.4 Example: Parser Combinators

As another example of using reflection, and of programming in Dart overall, we'll look at parser combinators. Parser combinators are operations that compose parsers out of other parsers. For example, consider a simple EBNF production for identifiers:

$$identifier \rightarrow letter(letter|digit)*$$

We will represent this production in Dart with the help of a parser combinator library, combinatorialParsing.dart. Using combinatorialParsing a parser for such identifiers can be built out of parsers that parse letters and parsers that parse digits:

```
var identifier =  letter & (letter | digit).star;
```

The Dart code is quite close to the EBNF specification. Assume letter is a parser that parses a single letter, and digit is parser that parses a single digit.

Parsers have several operators defined on them. One is |, which defines the *alternating combinator*. It takes a parser as its incoming argument, and returns a new parser that accepts whatever either the receiver or the argument accept. Hence, letter | digit will parse either a single letter or a single digit.

The alternating parser as presented here corresponds to the alternation operator in PEGs[18]. It differs from alternation in BNF in that it always give priority to its left side operand.[3]

Parsers also support the getter method star. The result of invoking star on a parser p is a new parser that will accept either the empty string or any number of repetitions of whatever p accepts. It follows that (letter | digit).star parses a sequence of zero or more characters that are either letters or digits.

Finally, the operator & is defined to return a new parser that parses whatever the receiver parses, and then parses whatever its argument parses. The net effect of letter & (letter | digit).star is to produce a parser object that parses a letter, and then accepts a (possibly empty) sequence of letters or digits.

The beauty of this scheme is that it is compositional in the same way the EBNF notation is. Effectively, we now have a domain-specific language for defining parsers that is very close to the high-level notation often used for grammars.

7.1.4.1 A Complete Grammar

We can define an entire grammar as a class where each production of the grammar is a member. The grammar is defined as a subclass of ExecutableGrammar, a class provided by combinatorialParsing. Individual parsers all have type CombinatorialParser:

```
class ExampleGrammar1 extends ExecutableGrammar {
    CombinatorialParser digit, letter, id, identifier, expression;
```

---

3. The implications of using PEGs vs. BNF are well beyond the scope of this book.

```
ExampleGrammar1() {
  digit = charBetween('0', '9');
  letter = charBetween('a', 'z') | charBetween('A', 'Z');
  id = letter & (letter | digit).star;
  identifier = tokenFor(id);
  expression = identifier;
}
}
```

The method charBetween() is inherited from ExecutableGrammar; it takes two one-element strings representing a contiguous range of characters and produces a parser that accepts any character in that range. And so digit is assigned a parser that accepts characters between "0" and "9", and letter is a parser that accepts either characters between "a" and "z" or between "A" and "Z", exactly as we'd expect.

The method tokenFor() is also inherited. It produces a tokenizing parser based on its input parser. The tokenizing parser will ignore whitespace. The framework therefore allows us to deal with both lexical and syntactic productions, producing a combined parser and scanner. This is known as scannerless parsing.

7.1.4.2 Grammar Subclassing and Mutual Recursion

Let us extend our grammar. The nice thing is that since grammars are classes, we can extend them just as we extend classes—via inheritance:

```
class ExampleGrammar2 extends ExampleGrammar1 {
  CombinatorialParser keywordIf, keywordThen, keywordElse, keywordReturn,
                      ifStatement, returnStatement, statement;
  ExampleGrammar2() {
    keywordIf = tokenFromSymbol('if');
    keywordThen = tokenFromSymbol('then');
    keywordElse = tokenFromSymbol('else');
    keywordReturn = tokenFromSymbol('return');
    returnStatement = keywordReturn & expression;
    ifStatement =
     keywordIf & expression & keywordThen &  statement & keywordElse & statement;
    statement = ifStatement | returnStatement;
  }
}
```

An interesting property of the above grammar is that it has mutually recursive productions. This is quite common in grammars, but it gives rise to a problem. When the ifStatement field is initialized, the getter for statement will be called, but it hasn't been initialized yet, so its value would be **null**. Changing the order of the field declarations won't help, because then the initialization of statement would attempt to invoke ifStatement that would be **null**. So how is the above code supposed to work?

One approach would be to disallow forward references, but this is simply unacceptable. Another tack is to specify productions via closures. In our case, it would be enough to define ifStatement as a closure.

    ifStatement =
        () => keywordIf & expression & keywordThen & statement & keywordElse
            & statement;

Of course, now the identifier ifStatement returns a closure rather than a parser, and one must call the function to extract the desired parser. We have to change how we refer to ifStatement:

    statement = ifStatement() | returnStatement;

These changes are problematic. Not all productions are represented the same way, which makes for confusion when referring to a production. One could decide to always use closures for productions, but the use of closures adds boilerplate code both at the definition of a production and at its use, making our internal DSL less attractive.

7.1.4.3 Forward Reference Parsers Using Reflection

We can solve this problem using reflection. We will initialize all fields of our grammar objects with special *forward reference parsers*. These parsers will support all the combinators supported by ordinary parsers so the initialization code can run without incident. When actual parsing commences, forward reference parsers look up the up-to-date value for the parser they refer to and parse accordingly.

The code to initialize fields to forward reference parsers is part of the parser combinator library. Specifically, the constructor for ExecutableGrammar sets all the fields of a grammar object to suitable forward reference parsers. Since the actual grammar is not known to the library, we need reflection to discover what those fields are and set them.

```
abstract class ExecutableGrammar extends CombinatorialParser {
    Map forwardReferenceTable = new Map();
    InstanceMirror selfMirror;
    ExecutableGrammar() {
        selfMirror = reflect(this);
        setupForwardReferences;
        bindForwardReferences;
    }
}
```

The constructor first obtains a mirror on the instance it is creating. The mirror is stored in selfMirror, where it is available to setUpForwardReferences, a routine that will assign forwarding parsers to all the instance variables of this. Initially, the forwarding parsers don't know what parser they will forward to; if we knew that when the forwarding parser was created, we wouldn't need a forwarding parser in the first place. Only after all the instance variables have been set by the constructor of the user-defined grammar can we actually bind each forwarding parser to the parser it should forward to.

Obviously, we need to be able to enumerate all the grammar's productions so we can assign forwarding parsers to their corresponding instance variables. We use a private utility method, _allProductions, to obtain these productions. It relies on reflection to go through all instance variables.

```
List<VariableMirror> get _allProductions {
    List<VariableMirror> allProductions = new List();
    ClassMirror gc = selfMirror.type;
    while (gc.simpleName != #ExecutableGrammar) {
        allProductions.addAll(gc.declarations.values.where(isInstanceField));
        gc = gc.superclass;
    }
    return allProductions;
}
```

The mirror library lets us enumerate the declarations of a single class. We need to climb up the type hierarchy in order to collect all the declarations. We climb the type hierarchy up to ExecutableGrammar. This allows us to collect all the fields defined by the user of the framework, and ignore the framework's own fields, which do not store parsers.

Using _allProductions, setupForwardReferences goes through all grammar productions, assigning a fresh instance of ForwardReferenceParser to each.

The actual parsers to be used will be defined in the subclass constructor's body, which will be run later. Clearly, as just noted, we do not know what parser each ForwardReferenceParser will forward to at this stage.

When the subclass constructor runs, it will assign the actual parsers to the various instance variables. As it does so, it will overwrite the forwarding parsers stored in each field. However, we will need to find the forwarding parsers later, to bind them to the real parsers. Therefore, as each ForwardReferenceParser is created, we store it in map, forwardReferenceTable, keyed by its field name.

```
get setupForwardReferences {
    /* go thru all instance variables and set them to a fresh forward reference */
    /* If these do not correspond to productions, they will be overridden by the subclass */
    for (VariableMirror slot in _allProductions){
        Symbol iv = slot.simpleName;
        var fref = new ForwardReferenceParser();
        /* Assume that all slots that are defined in subclasses of ExecutableGrammar
         * are productions. They will get overridden if they have another use.
         * Only if a field with the same name is defined by a subclass will this fail.
         * */
        forwardReferenceTable[iv] = fref;
        /* set iv to fref */
        selfMirror.setField(iv, fref);
    };
}
```

After the subclass constructor has run, we would like to bind the forwarding parsers to their targets. The problem is that at that point, the constructor for ExecutableGrammar will have already been executed, and we won't have an opportunity to traverse all the forwarding parsers to bind them.

To overcome this difficulty, every forwarding parser has a field bindingRoutine that holds onto a closure that will bind it to its target lazily. The first time a ForwardReferenceParser is asked to parse anything, it checks if it is already bound to its target; if not, it calls bindingRoutine.

In bindForwardReferences, we set the bindingRoutine field for all the forwarding parsers to the method finalBindForwardReferences:

```
// forward references
  get bindForwardReferences {
    for (var v in forwardReferenceTable.values) {
    v.bindingRoutine = () => finalBindForwardReferences;
    };
  }

    get finalBindForwardReferences {
       forwardReferenceTable.forEach((k, v){
      var p = getRealField(k);
      if (p is CombinatorialParser) {
          v.bind(p);
          p.name = MirrorSystem.getName(k);
          /* a good place to name the productions */
      }});
    }
```

The finalBindForwardReferences method actually binds all forwarding parsers, so in fact, it only gets called once, by the very first forwarding parser that needs to parse something. The method iterates through forwardReferenceTable, and sets each forwarding parser to the value stored in the corresponding field. Of course, this only works because finalBindForwardReferences is called after the grammar is fully set up.

We use reflection once more, in order to obtain the target parser we wish to bind to. That parser is stored in a field, whose name is the key to the map entry for the forwarding parser we are binding.

```
    CombinatorialParser getRealField(Symbol k){
     /*
      * If the current class has a getter k but not a field
      * then assume that its getter k overrides the production k stored
      * in a field in the superclass with a wrapping parser on the field contents.
      * */
     var p = selfMirror.getField(k).reflectee;
     if (selfMirror.type.getters.containsKey(k) &&
        selfMirror.type.declarations.values.where(isInstanceField).isEmpty))
       return p.parser;
```

```
        else return p;
}
```

7.1.4.4   Semantic Actions, ASTs and Deserialization

Our two previous examples, ExampleGrammar1 and ExampleGrammar2, both produce a
concrete parse tree. The parser combinators do this implicitly. The tree takes the form
of a list returned by the parser. In most cases, we want a parser to produce something
higher-level, such as an abstract syntax tree (AST).

We can do this by defining two classes: one defining the grammar for our language,
and a subclass that overrides some of the productions to produce the AST instead. Our
next example will illustrate this. We'll define the parser required for the deserializer of
the previous section. First, the grammar:

```
class SerializedObjectGrammar extends ExecutableGrammar {
  CombinatorialParser comma, decimal, digit, dot, doublequote, id, identifier,
                      integer, lbracket, letter, libName, list, literal, lparen,
                      nonliteral, number, rbracket, rparen, serializedObject, slash,
                      space, string, stringContent, sym, truth, underscore, untruth;


  SerializedObjectGrammar(){
      comma = token(',');
      dot = token('.');
      doublequote = token('"');
      lbracket = token('[');
      rbracket = token(']');
      lparen = token('(');
      rparen = token(')');
      slash = token('/');
      space = char(' ');
      underscore = char('_');
      digit = charBetween('0', '9');
      letter = charBetween('a', 'z') | charBetween('A', 'Z');
      integer = tokenFor(digit.plus);
      decimal = tokenFor(digit.plus & char('.') & digit.plus);
      number = decimal | integer;
      id = ((letter | underscore) & (letter | digit | underscore).star).wrapper(
           (fst, snd) => '$fst${new StringBuffer()..writeAll(snd)}'
      );
      identifier = tokenFor(id);
      truth = token('true');
      untruth = token('false');
      stringContent = (letter | digit | underscore | space).star;
```

```
    string = doublequote & stringContent & doublequote;
    sym =  token('Symbol') & lparen & doublequote & identifier
            & doublequote & rparen;
    literal = truth | untruth | number | sym | string;
    list = lbracket & integer.star & rbracket;
    libName = identifier & (dot & identifier).star;
    nonliteral = libName & slash & identifier & lparen & integer.star & rparen;
    serializedObject = literal | list | nonliteral;
  }
}
```

Next, we define a subclass of SerializedObjectGrammar that produces the AST. In our case, the AST is exceedingly simple. It consists of instances of SerializedObject and literals:

```
class SerializedObjectParser extends SerializedObjectGrammar {

  _computeIntFrom(List ints) {
    int val = 0;
    int j = 0;
    for (int i = ints.length-1; i >= 0; i-) {
      val += int.parse(ints[j++]) * math.pow(10, i);
    }
    return val;
  }

  _computeFractionFrom(List ints) {
    num val = 0;
    for (int i = 0;  i < ints.length; i++) {
      val += int.parse(ints[i]) / math.pow(10, i+1);
    }
    return val;
  }

  CombinatorialParser get integer {
    return super.integer.wrapper((Token ints) {return _computeIntFrom(ints.token);});
  }

  CombinatorialParser get truth => super.truth.wrapper((t) => true);
  CombinatorialParser get untruth => super.untruth.wrapper((f) => false);

  CombinatorialParser get decimal {
    return super.decimal.wrapper((d){
          return _computeIntFrom(d.token[0]) + _computeFractionFrom(d.token[2]);
        });
  }
}
```

```
CombinatorialParser get string {
    return super.string.wrapper((lq, s, rq){
        return s.fold('', (String s1, String s2) => s1 + s2);
    });
}

CombinatorialParser get sym {
    return super.sym.wrapper((f, lp, ldq, s, rdq, rp){
        return MirrorSystem.getSymbol(s.token);
    });
}

CombinatorialParser get libName {
    return super.libName.wrapper((Token hd, List tail) {
        List l = [hd.token];
        l.addAll(tail.map((List pair) => pair[0].token + pair[1].token));
        String ln = l.reduce((String s1, String s2) => s1 + s2);
        Symbol h = MirrorSystem.getSymbol(ln);
        return h;
    });
}

CombinatorialParser get nonliteral {
    return  super.nonliteral.wrapper(
            (Symbol libId, sl, Token classId, lp, List ints, rp) {
        Symbol c = MirrorSystem.getSymbol(classId.token);
        var dso = new serializer.SerializedObject(sid, libId, c);
        dso.fields = ints;
        return dso;
    });
}

CombinatorialParser get literal {
    return super.literal.wrapper((l) {
        return new serializer.SerializedLiteral(sid, l);
    });
}
```

```
CombinatorialParser get list {
  return super.list.wrapper((lb, elems, rb) {
      serializer.SerializedList res = new serializer.SerializedList(sid);
      res.fields = elems;
      return res;
    });
  }
}
```

7.1.4.5   Using noSuchMethod Instead of Reflection

As noted in Section 7.1.1 using reflection can carry a significant penalty. Is there another way for us to preserve the functionality of our library without resorting to reflection? Yes, there is. We can leverage noSuchMethod instead. This approach is illustrated by class RunnableGrammar:

```
abstract class RunnableGrammar extends CombinatorialParser {
  Map<Symbol, ForwardReferenceParser> forwardReferenceTable =
      new Map<Symbol, ForwardReferenceParser>();
  Map<Symbol, dynamic> productions = new Map<Symbol, dynamic>();
  // non-parsers might be inserted by noSuchMethod,
  // so values have type dynamic
  RunnableGrammar();


  noSuchMethod(Invocation im){
    // if it's a get, look it up in the productions map;
    // if it's missing, install a forwarder and return that
    if (im.isGetter) {
      var result;
      return (result = productions[im.memberName]) == null ?
        setupForwardReference(im.memberName): result;
    };
    // if it is a set, install in the productions map
    if (im.isSetter){
      // Must be careful, since setter name and getter name differ by trailing '='!
      String setterName = MirrorSystem.getName(im.memberName);
      Symbol fieldName =
        new Symbol(setterName.substring(0, setterName.length - 1));
      return productions[fieldName] = im.positionalArguments[0];
    };
    // otherwise forward to super method
    return super.noSuchMethod(im);
  }
```

```
ForwardReferenceParser setupForwardReference(Symbol productionName){
  ForwardReferenceParser fref =  new ForwardReferenceParser();
  fref.bindingRoutine = () => finalBindForwardReferences;
  return productions[productionName] =
              forwardReferenceTable[productionName] = fref;
}


// forward references
  get finalBindForwardReferences {
      forwardReferenceTable.forEach((k, v){
        var p = productions[k];
        if (p is CombinatorialParser) {
          v.bind(p);
          p.name = MirrorSystem.getName(k);
          /* a good place to name the productions */
        }});
  }
}
```

Here, the heart of the process is in noSuchMethod(). Productions are stored in a map, productions, from production names to parsers. Any attempt to set a production causes its value to be inserted into the production map. When a production is referenced, it is looked up in the production map. If the production was not a forward reference, it will already have been set. If it is absent, a forwarding parser is created and added to the map and to forwardReferenceTable.

One advantage of this scheme is that we need not declare a field for each production as we did before. We simply reference the setters and getters for the productions in the constructor:

```
class ExampleGrammar3 extends RunnableGrammar {
    ExampleGrammar3() {
      digit = charBetween('0', '9');
      letter = charBetween('a', 'z') | charBetween('A', 'Z');
      id = letter & (letter | digit).star;
      identifier = tokenFor(id);
      expression = identifier;
    }
}
```

We also no longer have to rely on reflection, which means that if we deploy to Javascript, our download will be smaller.

However, we lose the advantages of type checking. Furthermore, actual parsing will be slower, as all access to productions goes through noSuchMethod, which can be significantly slower than an ordinary getter invocation.

Overall, reflection would probably be a better choice on a Dart VM, but using noSuchMethod might be preferable when deploying via Javascript. And of course, one might choose an entirely different approach, such as an external DSL. A promising alternative is to use a reflection library that supports code generation; we'll examine that option in Section 7.4.

7.2 Why Mirrors

Dart uses mirror-based reflection. There are alternative approaches to handling reflection in a language. Why does Dart opt to use mirrors?

It is often said that every problem in computing can be solved by adding a level of indirection. Mirrors are a case in point.

Mirrors help deployment of reflective code and libraries; by moving reflective functionality into a separate component, it becomes easier to recognize whether reflection is being used, and therefore whether the reflection code needs to be preserved in the deployed code.

Mirrors are useful when reflecting in a distributed system. In contrast to the approaches where one reflects by directly handling actual implementation artifacts like classes, mirrors allow different implementations to be supported simultaneously. In particular, one can support implementations of mirrors that act as proxies for code and objects in a separate address space, be it another actor, process or a remote machine.

As distinct objects, mirrors act as capabilities for reflection, and are thus a natural fit for an object-capability security model.

The first two considerations are germane to Dart; the last is not, because Dart bases its security on isolates. For a more detailed discussion of mirrors, see the related work section at the end of this Chapter (7.6).

7.3 Metadata

Declarations in Dart can be decorated with *metadata annotations*. Metadata is given before a declaration. A metadata annotation starts with an at sign (@) followed by either a reference to a constant variable or a call to a constant constructor. Several annotations may be given:

```
@deprecated prematureOptimization(x) { ... }
@specialToLib1 @ImportantToLib2(4) class MyClass {
  @override toString() => 'I am in a class of my own';
}
```

Metadata can be accessed at runtime via reflection. The class DeclarationMirror in dart:mirrors has a getter, metadata, which returns a list of mirrors on the values of the various annotations associated with the declaration.

If metadata is not accessed dynamically, it should incur no overhead; a good implementation will ignore metadata until it is requested. Since metadata is made up exclusively of constants, its value is independent of the program state, and so it can be computed at any time with identical results. In particular, metadata can be evaluated on demand, avoiding any overhead for unused annotations.

In many cases, metadata need not be accessed dynamically at all. Tools can parse code statically, off line, and take advantage of metadata annotations as they see fit.

We shall now look at an example that accesses metadata reflectively to some advantage.

7.4   Reflection via Code Generation

As noted above, using reflection when deploying to a platform that does not support a proper Dart virtual machine (e.g., the web or iOS) can be costly in terms of space. In many cases, we can adapt our code to deal with this problem.

To prevent an explosion in the size of the deployed application, the implementation needs to know what code is being accessed reflectively, and how. To this end, Dart supports an alternative mirror library, **reflectable**. Reflectable requires code that will be reflected upon to be annotated with specific metadata. The metadata describes what capabilities must be supported when reflecting upon the annotated code. For example, whether one should be able to reflectively invoke members of the class, or analyze their structure, or traverse the class' supertype chain etc.

We will illustrate the use of **reflectable** using the parser combinator library shown above.

Ideally, once the requisite annotations are in place, the deployed code should function as intended while being a lot smaller. In practice, there are still incompatibilities between **reflectable** and **dart:mirrors**. We will therefore have to make some small adjustments to the code.

Our first step is to import **reflectable**, and to import its mirror library rather than the standard one.

```
import 'package:reflectable/reflectable.dart' show
                   declarationsCapability, instanceInvokeCapability, Reflectable,
                   TypeCapability, typeRelationsCapability;
import 'package:reflectable/mirrors.dart' show ClassMirror, InstanceMirror, Mirror,
                                               VariableMirror;
```

The next step is to define the set of reflective capabilities that we need. For example, we require the capability to reflectively obtain the type of an instance of a grammar. Reflectable defines the class TypeCapability for this purpose. Specifically, the constructor of TypeCapability takes a constant Type t as an argument, and produces an object representing the capability to reflectively obtain the type of instances of t:

```
const grammarTypeCapability = const TypeCapability(ExecutableGrammar);
```

Reflectable also provides predefined constants for some common capabilities. Here, we use declarationsCapability, typeRelationsCapability and instanceInvokeCapability. The first allows us to access the structure of a class, the second allows us to reflectively traverse the type hierarchy, and the last enables reflectively calling instance members.

To utilize capabilities, we need to create a mirror system that has them. Reflectable's mirror systems are instances of subclasses of class **Reflectable**. We'll define class **Grammar** to describe a mirror system that supports the capabilities an executable grammar needs:

```
const grammar = const Grammar();
```

```
class Grammar extends Reflectable {
  const Grammar() : super(declarationsCapability,
  instanceInvokeCapability,
  typeRelationsCapability,
  grammarTypeCapability);
}
```

We'll need to annotate grammar classes with @grammar, thereby letting reflectable know that those classes must be accessible via reflection, in accordance with the capabilities specified for Grammar (the class of grammar).

```
@grammar abstract class ExecutableGrammar extends CombinatorialParser {...}
```

There are also a few API incompatibilities between dart:mirrors and reflectable/mirrors. The methods getField and setField in dart:mirrors are misnomers. In reflectable these are renamed to invokeGetter and invokeSetter, respectively.[4] We'll need to change our code in a few places:

```
CombinatorialParser getRealField(String k){
    /* A gross hack to work around the deficiencies in Dart's mirror lib.
     * If the current class has a getter k but not a field
     * then assume that its getter k overrides the production k stored
     * in a field in the superclass with a wrapping parser on the field contents.
     * */
    var p = selfMirror.invokeGetter(k);
    if (selfMirror.type.instanceMembers.containsKey(k) &&
       selfMirror.type.declarations.values.where(isInstanceField).isEmpty)
      return p.parser;
    else return p;
}
```

```
get setupForwardReferences {
    /* go thru all non-nil instance variables and set them to a fresh forward reference */
    /* If these do not correspond to productions, they will be overridden by the subclass */
```

---

4. Future versions of dart:mirrors will correct this problem.

```
_allProductions.forEach((VariableMirror slot){
  String iv = slot.simpleName;
  var fref =  new ForwardReferenceParser();
  forwardReferenceTable[iv] = fref;
  /* set iv to fref */
  selfMirror.invokeSetter(iv, fref);
});
}
```

In addition, reflectable uses strings rather than symbols to name declarations. Given that reflectable already deals with deployment, it is not concerned with optimizing for minification. This makes it easier to use.

```
List<VariableMirror> get _allProductions {
  List<VariableMirror> allProductions = new List();
  ClassMirror gc = selfMirror.type;
  while (gc.simpleName != 'ExecutableGrammar') {
    allProductions.addAll(gc.declarations.values.where(isInstanceField));
    gc = gc.superclass;
  }
  return allProductions;
}
```

Finally, we need to annotate our client code with grammar as well:[5]

```
import 'parsing.dart' show CombinatorialParser, ExecutableGrammar,  grammar;

@grammar class ExampleGrammar1 extends ExecutableGrammar {..}
```

We can run our example as before. By default, reflectable uses dart:mirrors behind the scenes. However, we can build a version of our application that has been optimized for deployment based on the reflection-capability annotations we've provided. The result is greatly reduced in size (an order of magnitude for our example). Compression yields almost another order of magnitude reduction.[6]

A reasonable strategy is to develop an application using dart:mirrors and to deploy it using reflectable. In fact, reflectable can be used directly on a Dart runtime, in which case it forwards its work to dart:mirrors. So we could write the application using reflectable from the start. The downside is that we would need to specify the reflective capabilities early in the process. However, we could specify the required capabilities gradually as we built the application. The upside is that we would not need to convert the application. We expect that using the Reflectable package will become an increasingly popular option as it matures and becomes more complete.

---

5. In fact, reflectable has a way of avoiding this but it is not yet implemented.

6. At the time of this writing, for our parsing example, we see a reduction of the translated Javascript code size from over 2Mb to 174Kb, which further compresses down to 30Kb.

7.5   Beyond Introspection

Some of the most exciting applications of reflection are those that involve reflective change—modifying or adding code on the fly. The primary use case for reflective change is during development. A system that supports reflective change makes it much easier to implement a live IDE.

It has always been the intent that Dart would support reflective change. At the time of this writing, only one, experimental, Dart implementation (code-named Fletch) supports this feature. We expect this to change over time, however.

The most obvious application of reflective change during development is that it enables live evaluators. These can be as basic as classic read-eval-print loops (REPLs) but can also be richer, for example, object inspectors that allow evaluation in the scope of a particular instance. Another standard use of reflective change is "fix-and-continue" debugging. It is worth noting that a true live environment allows modification of declarations of all kinds, not just methods and functions. One should be able to add, remove or rename fields and have the changes take effect immediately on all existing instances, for example.

When adding or renaming a field, one has to consider how it might be initialized. A reflective change facility should provide means of updating existing instances so that they not only have the declared slots, but that the slots have appropriate values.

The use of reflective change in production is much more controversial. An example of such use would be a programmer-defined version of dynamic loading. Another is optimizing designs based on noSuchMethod, such as proxies. One can add custom versions of methods when they are first invoked, avoiding the overhead of noSuchMethod calls on later invocations (at the cost of large overhead on the first call). Perhaps most intriguingly, one might choose to update deployed applications on the fly, without needing to restart them.

However, supporting reflective change in production does raise issues. One can no longer be certain what the code of an application is, and one might have security concerns. The performance demands on the reflective-change machinery are higher as well.

7.6   Related Work

The history of reflection in object-oriented programming is rooted in Smalltalk. Variants of the Smalltalk model were adopted in other languages. CLOS enriched it with the metaobject protocol, whereas Java restricted it, and C# followed suit.

Later scripting languages supported reflection in an unstructured fashion by deliberately exposing implementation structure to the programmer. In this, they followed in the tradition of metacircular Lisp systems that predated Smalltalk.

The notion of mirrors was introduced in Self[19]. The Self model was adapted to class-based systems, first in Strongtalk, and later in parts of the Java platform such as

JDI and APT. For extensive discussion, see [20]. More recently, Newspeak introduced a mirror system intent on realizing the full benefits outlined in [20]. The Dart mirror system is a descendant of the Newspeak design, but differs in many respects. Dart's inter-isolate communication differs from Newspeak's, causing the forking of the API into local and inter-isolate versions. Dart must deal with deployment constraints specific to the web platform, leading to a reliance on constant symbols and annotations. The Dart mirror API has yet to evolve to deal with live program modifications and debugging support.

The parser combinator library shown here is based on the Newspeak version first described in [21].

Metadata became popular in .Net, and was consequently introduced into Java. Dart metadata is unique in that it leverages constants.

7.7   Summary

Mirrors locate reflective functionality outside of the objects being reflected, offering the promise of better support for deployment, distribution and security than older reflective APIs. Dart mirrors currently support introspection and the ability to reflectively run code; in future, we hope to provide the ability to modify live programs as well.

Chapter 8

Asynchrony and Isolates

We have focused on sequential Dart programs until now. However, most real Dart programs are concurrent.

A web application usually consists of at least two concurrent parts—a client program running in a web browser on a user's device, and a server program running outside the browser, usually on another computer somewhere across the internet. Many server side programs service many clients simultaneously. These are typical scenarios, but there are many others.

In this chapter, we shall turn our attention to the those features of Dart that support concurrency and distribution. Dart concurrency is based on isolates (8.4), which in turn are built upon futures (8.2) and streams (8.3).

8.1 Asynchrony

When one invokes a method or calls a function in Dart, the caller waits until the callee has been evaluated and returns a result. While the callee is executing, the caller is *blocked*. A function call is much like a phone call, where the caller waits for the other party to answer. Calling is a form of *synchronous* communication—caller and callee synchronize their activity in time.

In contrast, in *asynchronous* communication the caller initiates an action but does not wait for it to complete, instead continuing execution immediately. Examples of situations where asynchronous communication might be appropriate include tasks like input or output, where the action requested might be slow and waiting for the action to complete is undesirable.

Asynchrony is fundamental to Dart's approach to concurrency. Dart supports asynchrony both within a single isolate and across multiple isolates.

Cross-isolate communication is based on asynchronous message passing. In its basic form, message-passing is a "fire-and-forget" activity. The sender has no assurance that the message was received or that a response will ever be given. This is analogous to sending a letter by old-fashioned post. One can initiate some action by sending a message, but one does not know if the action was carried out, and if so if it was successful or not. One certainly cannot tell what the resulting value was in case of success, nor what error was thrown in case of failure. This is unsatisfactory. Applications need to be able to monitor and respond to the asynchronous activities they initiate. To address this need, we use futures.

8.2   Futures

A *future* is an object that represents the result of a computation that may not yet have taken place. The result may be known at some future time, hence the name "future." Futures are useful in asynchronous computation. Once a request to perform an asynchronous computation is made, a future can be returned immediately, in a synchronous fashion, and the actual computation can be scheduled for a later time. The future gives the code requesting the asynchronous operation a handle, a reference to the requested computation. After the requested computation is completed, the future can be used to get access to the result. We say that the future *has been completed*, or alternatively, *has been resolved*.

In Dart, futures are realized by the class Future in the dart:async library. Future is a generic class (5.5), with type parameter T representing the type of value the future will be completed with.

8.2.1   Consuming Futures

Futures have an instance method then() that takes a closure, onValue, as a parameter. This closure will be called when the future completes successfully. The closure itself takes a parameter of type T, the type of the computation the future represents. So, when the future is complete, the value it represents will be passed to onValue.

As an example, suppose we have a file that we wish to copy. File[1] objects support an asynchronous API for copying files:

    Future<File> copy(String newPath)

If we call copy() on a File, we get a future back. An advantage of the asynchronous API is that one can initiate a copy of a large file and not wait for the copying to complete. The downside is that if we actually want to do something with the copy, things get a bit more complicated because we must interact with futures.

A simple test might assert that if we have a file and make a copy at a path myPath, the resulting file's path is indeed myPath. Because the result of copy() is a future on a file rather than the file itself, we can't just write

    assert(myFile.copy(myPath).path == myPath);

The correct code is

    myFile.copy(myPath).then((f){assert(f.path == myPath);});

After the file system is done copying, the future returned by copy() will be completed with an actual File object, and the closure passed into then() will be called with said

---

1. Here we refer to the File class defined in dart:io, as opposed to the one defined in dart:html which has a different API altogether.

File instance, causing the assertion to fire. By that time, Dart execution will have long since moved on.

What if a future f_1 represents a computation that results in another future f_2? It won't do to have f_1 complete if the result is itself a future. We would call onValue but be forced to test if the incoming argument was a future and deal with that via another then() and so on ad infinitum. Instead, in such cases the completion of f_1 is made dependent on the completion of f_2. When f_2 is completed with a non-future value, f_1 will complete with the same value. We say the futures are *chained* because they form a dependency chain.

Futures can represent failed computations as well. The method catchError() is also defined on futures, and it too takes a closure as input. The closure, onError, is invoked if the computation the future represents throws an exception.

8.2.2 Producing Futures

In principle, code that needs to return a future to its caller must do several things. It must schedule a computation to be executed at some later time, it must instantiate an instance of Future and it must associate that instance with the scheduled computation, so that when the scheduled computation is done, the future will be completed with the result. Care must be taken to catch any exceptions the scheduled computation throws and complete the future with the appropriate errors.

The constructors of Future manage all this bookkeeping for us. The code looks roughly like this:

```
Future(Function computation){
  Timer.run(() =>
    try {
      _completeWithValue(computation());
    }
    catch (e){
      _completeWithError(e);
  });
}
```

The class Timer, defined in dart:async, has a static method run() that schedules code for execution. The Future constructor takes a closure computation embodying the computation the user wants to schedule. The actual job scheduled, however, is a closure designed to capture the result of computation, successful or otherwise, and complete the instance of Future being constructed as appropriate. The completion is done via private methods such as _completeWithValue(). We do not want to expose these to the consumers of futures; such consumers need not, and should not, be able to influence the results of the future instance returned to them.

The net effect is that the Dart programmer simply writes something like:

```
new Future(myComputation);
```

where myComputation defines the computation desired.

8.2.3 Scheduling

When we say that code is scheduled for future execution, what do we mean? A Dart application has an event loop that is run as long as there are *event handlers* available to process ongoing events. Event handlers target a variety of events—mouse clicks, keyboard input and others. Of particular interest to us are timer events—events that mark the passage of time.

The class Timer mentioned in the previous section is used to define handlers for timer events. One can define a handler that is designed to trigger after a given time period has elapsed. An important special case is when that time period is zero. A handler that triggers when zero time has passed is simply a task that we want to run unconditionally at the earliest opportunity. One can define such a handler using Timer.run(). Setting up such a handler amounts to scheduling a task for future execution, to be run in a subsequent iteration of the event loop.

It is possible to schedule a future to execute after a non-zero delay, via the constructor Future.delayed(). See the Dart API documentation for details on this and the several other constructors for futures.

Once a task is started, it runs to completion; tasks are never preempted. The period in which a task is run is called a *turn*. All futures scheduled within a turn are guaranteed to be run only after the turn is finished—except for microtasks, described below.

8.2.3.1 Microtasks

As a rule, we must also assume that other code might execute before a task we have scheduled via a future. That code might be

- Code from another isolate

- An event handler associated with an event such as a mouse click

- The computation associated with other futures scheduled previously

Any one of the above kinds of tasks could be run by the event loop once the current turn is over, before any future scheduled by the current turn gets to run. Sometimes, we really need to run some asynchronous action before the event loop resumes.

There is a mechanism for ensuring that a future runs before any code scheduled outside our turn. Each turn has its own *microtask queue*. Tasks on the microtask queue are run at the end of the turn before returning control to the main event loop.

We can schedule futures to run on the microtask queue using the constructor Future.microtask(). It is important to keep microtasks few and short.

8.3 Streams

A *stream* is a list of values of indeterminate length. It may be infinite, going on forever. Or it may end eventually, but the point is that we don't know when or if the stream ends.

Examples of streams might be the position of the mouse over time, or a list of all prime numbers, or a live video being sent to us over the network.

One may *subscribe* (or *listen*) to a stream, meaning that one registers one or more callback functions with the stream. These functions will be called when new data is appended to the stream.

It is natural to view a stream as a collection. Many operations on collections apply to streams. One can invoke map() on a stream and thereby derive a transformed stream of computed results. For example, we can map a pair of coordinates to an image translated by those coordinates, and thus build an application that moves an image around the scene in response to mouse movements.

A stream derived using map() is 1:1 with the original stream from which it is derived. Sometimes it is useful to be able to replace an element of the stream with multiple elements. As a special case, if that multiple is 0, we can filter out elements. The expand() operation (known as flatMap() in many other languages) allows us to do so.

Filtering elements can be done using expand() but it is easier to use where().

Some operations on collections need to traverse the entire collection. In the case of streams, we cannot do so immediately, so these operations return futures. For example, suppose we had a stream primes of all prime numbers and we wanted to sum them up:

```
Future<int> sisypheanSum = sum(primes);
sisypheanSum.then((s) => print(s));
```

Of course, this is a rather Sisyphean task if our stream of primes really keeps running forever. If our stream does shut down at some point, then we will get a result. What is nice is that the same sum() function we used back in Section 4.4 will work unchanged with a stream.

8.4   Isolates

Dart supports *actor-style concurrency*. A running Dart program consists of one or more actors, known as *isolates*. An isolate is a computation with its own memory and its own single thread of control. The term *isolate* derives from the isolation that exists between isolates, because an isolate's memory is logically separate from the memory of any other isolate. Code within an isolate runs sequentially; any concurrency is a result of running multiple isolates. Hence there is no shared memory concurrency in Dart, and therefore no need for locks and no possibility of races.

Since isolates have no shared memory, the only way that isolates can communicate is via message passing. Message passing in Dart is always asynchronous.

Unlike some languages, isolates have no blocking receive construct. As a result, deadlock cannot occur.

8.4.1   Ports

An isolate has several *ports*. Ports are the low-level foundation upon which Dart's inter-isolate communication is built. Ports are of two kinds: *send port* and *receive ports*.

A receive port is a stream (8.3) of incoming messages. A send port allows messages to be sent to an isolate; more specifically, it allows messages to be posted to a receive port. Receive ports can manufacture send ports that post any messages sent on them to their originating receive port. We'll see how this works in the next subsection.

8.4.2 Spawning

Starting up one isolate from another is known as *spawning*. An isolate begins execution at the main() method of a library that is specified when the isolate is spawned. This library is called the *root library* of the isolate.

The class Isolate provides two class methods for spawning. The first is spawnUri(), which spawns an isolate based on a library given via a URI. The second is spawn(), which produces an isolate based on the current isolate's root library.

A Dart program begins execution in the *main isolate*, spawned by the Dart runtime. In order to create new isolates, the code running in the main isolate will have to spawn them. When an isolate spawns another, it has the opportunity to pass some initial arguments. The most critical such argument is an initial *message*. Messages are defined inductively: a message is either **null**, a number, a Boolean, a string, a send port, a list of messages or a map from messages to messages. The initial message typically includes a send port that the newly spawned isolate (the *spawnee*) will use to send messages back to the isolate that spawned it (its *spawner*).

How does the spawner produce a send port to pass to its spawnee? The spawner creates its receive port r_1, extracts a send port s_1 from it and spawns a new isolate, passing in the new send port:

```
main() { // in the main isolate
  ReceivePort r1 = new ReceivePort();
  SendPort s1 = r1.sendPort;
  Isolate.spawnUri(new Uri(path:'./otherIsolate.dart'), [], s1);
}
```

The spawnee then creates its own receive port r_2, and extracts a send port s_2 from it, which gets sent back to the spawner via s_1. This mating dance results in a pair of isolates that can communicate with each other:

```
main(args, SendPort s1) { // in otherIsolate.dart
  ReceivePort r2 = new ReceivePort();
  SendPort s2 = r2.sendPort;
  s1.send(s2);
}
```

The process just described is a bit tedious, though it only amounts to three lines of ritualistic code at the start of each isolate. However, the port mechanism is sufficiently flexible that various higher-level mechanisms can be built on top of it, as we shall soon see.

8.4.3 Security

Isolates are the foundation of security in Dart. Memory isolation prevents one isolate from impacting the state of another. As a result, the language's privacy constructs have no security implications, and serve only software engineering purposes.

One consequence is that one can violate the privacy of libraries via reflection (7), and that reflection is unrestricted within the confines of an isolate. Cross-isolate reflection is another matter.

8.5 Example: Client-Server Communication

In this section, we will show how to structure a web application in a way that is independent of the specific mechanics of the web browser. We will view the application as a pair of communicating isolates, one representing the server and one representing the client.

We will take the view that the server is itself an object with an interface of operations it makes available to the client. These operations will all be asynchronous, returning futures. However, the futures returned will be of a special kind we shall now define, which we shall call *promises*.

8.5.1 Promise: A Brighter Future

Promises are designed to mitigate the pain of interacting with asynchronous code. Promises handle the boilerplate of call-backs on futures automatically. Using noSuch-Method(), a promise transforms method invocations made on it into callbacks using then().

When a method invocation returns a promise, one can immediately invoke further methods on the promise, almost as if it was the actual result. This alleviates much of the tedium of using futures, as code is no longer full of deeply nested callback declarations.

```dart
library promise;
import 'dart:async' show Completer, Future;
import 'dart:mirrors' show InstanceMirror, reflect;
@proxy class Promise {
  Future _future;
  Promise(this._future);
  noSuchMethod(Invocation inv) {
    onValue(v) {
      InstanceMirror m = reflect(v);
      var result = m.delegate(inv);
      return result;
    }
    return new Promise(_future.then(onValue));
  }
}
```

```
class Resolver {
  Completer _completer = new Completer();
  Promise _promise;
  get promise {
    return _promise == null ? _promise = new Promise(_completer.future): _promise;
  }
  resolve(v) {
    _completer.complete(v);
  }
}
```

8.5.1.1   Limitations: Promises We Can't Keep

The code above suffers from the same problem we saw before for general-purpose proxies (5.7.6). The difference between a promise and the actual value will be detected by dynamic type checks—both explicit checks and casts (via **is** and **as**) and implicit checks in checked mode.

The process also breaks down when the results are needed by control constructs such as conditionals and loops, or for output. Compare printing of a known value v to printing a promise p for v:

```
print(v); // prints the value v
print(p); // prints something like 'An instance of Promise'
```

The immediate problem here is that print() relies on toString(), which is inherited from Object. A more thorough forwarding mechanism would override all the methods of Object and forward them, via then() to the future. However, that doesn't really solve the problem in this case; instead it aggravates it. If print() gets a Promise back from toString() instead of a string as expected, it will throw an exception.

Even more acute is the issue of control flow. If we have an asynchronous predicate, we cannot use its result to make a control flow decision in a conditional.[2]

We could try adding methods that emulate conditionals, essentially deferring the decisions on control flow until the promise is resolved. However, these methods will not properly handle constructs like **break, continue** and **return**.

Finally, there is some concern over performance. Calls using noSuchMethod() may be significantly slower than normal calls and so one needs to take care that they are not used in performance critical code. This should not be a concern for the scenario we have in mind, where remote isolates are communicating. A potentially more serious worry is that using noSuchMethod() makes code harder to analyze statically, which tends to increase code size when compiling to Javascript.

Despite all the above problems, promises can be useful in certain circumstances. In the following sections, we shall look at using promises in the context of client-server communication.

---

2. The issues with respect to output and control flow are fundamentally the same. These are in essence *strict* functions that will not accept lazy inputs.

8.5.2   Isolates as Distributed Objects

Our next step is to provide a view of isolates as objects. We will need to define the service API as a Dart class, write code to run the service from a client, and of course implement the service. Last but not least, we'll need to build the infrastructure used by the service and its clients.

8.5.2.1   Service API

Assume we have a service that lets people send cookies to a given address. The API for this service is very simple, and is given by the following abstract class:

```
abstract class CookieService {
    Receipt sendCookiesTo(recipientAddress, customer);
}
```

You tell the service where to send the cookies, and give them your details so they can charge you. The service returns a receipt once it processes the request (they charge you right away, not when the cookies ship).

Object Serialization.   Our model relies on sending objects between client and server, which entails object serialization. We assume that all objects being serialized are instances of types that are known to both the client and the server. We also assume these types are exactly the same on both ends of the connection.

8.5.2.2   Running the Service

To run the service, we define our main isolate via the library:

```
library drive_cookie_service;

import 'civilisolates.dart' as civilisolates show startServiceObject;
```

We rely on the library civilisolates to provide the necessary infrastructure, specifically the method startService used below:

```
main() {
  var cookieService =
          civilisolates.startServiceObject(new Uri(path: 'cookie_service.dart'));
  cookieService.sendCookies(getAddress(), getCustomerDetails());
}
```

The code above starts up a service based upon the library at cookie_service.dart using startServiceObject. The effect of startServiceObject is to start up an isolate based on the library at the URI passed to it, and return a promise that allows us to communicate with the new isolate.

Next, we invoke sendCookies() on the promise, which we stored in the local variable cookieService. The service isolate probably hasn't even started up yet, but no matter;

because startServiceObject returns a promise, not just a plain future, we can immediately invoke the method sendCookies() on it.

All the client needed to do is reference the service via a URI. After that, it talks to the service as an ordinary object. As we'll see, the situation on the server side is also quite simple.

8.5.2.3   Service Implementation

To implement our service, we define cookie_service.dart as follows:

```
library cookie_service;

import 'civilisolates.dart' as civilisolates show serve;

class MyCookieService implements CookieService {
  Receipt sendCookiesTo(recipientAddress, customer){
    charge(customer); // first things first
    initiatePhysicalShipment(recipientAddress);
    return new Receipt(customer);
  }
}

main(args, client) {
  CookieService obj = new MyCookieService();
  civilisolates.serve(obj, client);
}
```

Again, we import civilisolates to provide necessary infrastructure. The cookie_service library defines a class MyCookieService with a set of operations that define the API of the service the library provides. To make the library act as a service, we instantiate MyCookieService and pass it to civilisolates.serve(). The call to serve() will make the currently running isolate listen for messages from client, convert them into method invocations on service, and send the serialized results back; in short, serve makes the current isolate act as a service implemented by obj.

Almost all our code is independent of asynchrony. We defined the functionality needed in an ordinary class. On the server side, only main() is slightly special—but it is mercifully brief and formulaic.

Of course, this picture is a bit oversimplified. Our promises don't work as smoothly if we have complex control flow that relies on results from an asynchronous call. We do have to design the API of our isolate at a suitable granularity to avoid these problems and to minimize round trips. But we have avoided a great deal of boilerplate code.

8.5.2.4   Infrastructure

Now let's look at the infrastructure we've been using to define and launch our service. This includes the definitions of startService and serve. It's all defined in the civilisolates library.

```
library civilisolates;

import 'dart:isolate' show Isolate, ReceivePort, SendPort;
import 'dart:async' show Completer, Future;
import 'dart:mirrors' show InstanceMirror, reflect;
import 'promise.dart' show Promise, Resolver;
import 'serializer.dart' as serializer show serialize;
import 'deserializer.dart' as deserializer show deserialize;

msg2Obj(List<String> msg) => deserializer.deserialize(msg);
List<String> obj2Msg(obj) => serializer.serialize(obj);
```

We'll make use of the serializer we introduced in Section 7.1.3. A more robust realization of these ideas would of course require better serialization support, but what we have suffices to illustrate the main ideas.

Below, you can see how **serve** helps an isolate represent an object (obj) as a service to a given client (represented via the send port client). It sets up the necessary ports to communicate with the client. It then listens for any incoming messages and forwards them using reflection to obj, sending the results back to the client:

```
void serve(obj, SendPort client) {
  // send client our address
  ReceivePort rport = new ReceivePort();
  SendPort selfPort = rport.sendPort;
  client.send(selfPort);
  // set up listener to respond to sends from client
  InstanceMirror target = reflect(obj);
  rport.listen (
    (msg){
      var invArgs = msg[0];
      SendPort returnAddress = msg[1];
      // forward invocation to obj
    var result = target.invoke(invArgs[0], msg2Obj(invArgs[1]), msg2Obj(invArgs[2]));
      // extract and serialize result and send back to client
      returnAddress.send(obj2Msg(result.reflectee));
    }
  );
}
```

Next, startServiceObject is used by clients to set up an object representing a service. The service will be implemented by a library residing at uri. We will use an isolate that will run our service. We begin with the mechanics of hooking up ports and spawning the service isolate. We want to create a proxy object for the isolate, but the isolate is created asynchronously. All we have is a future for a send port for the isolate. And so, we return a promise for the proxy instead. When the future for the port completes, it will trigger creation of the proxy:

```
Promise startServiceObject(uri) {
  ReceivePort rport = new ReceivePort();
  SendPort selfPort = rport.sendPort;
  // start up the service isolate
  Isolate.spawnUri(uri, [], selfPort);
  // When we get the isolates address back
  // we can set up a proxy object for it. In the meantime,
  // return a promise for the proxy
    Future<SendPort> target = rport.elementAt(0);
    return new Promise(target.then((s) => new IsolateProxy(s)));
}
```

The last piece of the puzzle is the proxy for isolates. It works similarly to the proxies we've seen before. The difference is in what the noSuchMethod routine does. It has to create a port specifically to listen for the answer to the method invocation it is currently handling. Each invocation gets its own port because we don't want to mix up the answers as they come back.

The invocation is serialized and sent to the target, the isolate being proxied. We return a promise for the result. We set up a listener to await the answer; the handler will resolve the promise to the deserialized answer when it arrives.

As a simplification we choose not to handle named parameters. Our example doesn't call for them, and our sample serialization code doesn't support maps:

```
class IsolateProxy {
  final SendPort _sendPort;
  IsolateProxy(this._sendPort);
  noSuchMethod(Invocation inv) {
    ReceivePort rport = new ReceivePort();
    // create a dedicated port to receive the answer for this invocation
    SendPort selfPort = rport.sendPort;
    Resolver resolver = new Resolver();
    //  When the answer comes, we'll be listening
    rport.listen((answer){
      // deserialize the answer;
      // first element of serialized form is the desired result
      var a = msg2Obj(answer)[0];
      // resolved promise accordingly
      resolver.resolve(a);
      // and shut down the port dedicated to this invocation
      rport.close();
    });
    // serialize the invocation and send it to the target isolate
    _sendPort.send([obj2Msg([inv.memberName, inv.positionalArguments]), selfPort]);
    return resolver.promise;
  }
}
```

One can of course create a proxy directly given a send port for an isolate; one doesn't have to use startServiceObject. It is merely a convenience in the case where we start up the service for the first time.

Unfortunately, chained promises as illustrated have limited utility in Dart for all the reasons cited in Section 8.5.1.1 above. To address these limitations, Dart has dedicated support for asynchrony at the language level, as we'll show next.

8.6 Asynchronous Functions

As we've seen, working directly with futures can be awkward. Part of the problem is that the classic control structures we are familiar with were not designed with asynchrony in mind. Once an asynchronous call has been made, all the bookkeeping necessary to track whether the call has executed, whether execution was successful or not and what were the results, becomes the responsibility of the programmer. The work of scheduling futures, and scheduling work to be done when that work is done, successfully or not, is rather onerous.

To ease the pain of working with asynchrony, Dart provides language-level support for asynchronous functions. A function body can be marked with the **async** modifier; the function is then an *async function*:

```
Future<int> foo() async => 42;
```

Using **async** functions can simplify the task of working with futures and asynchrony in several ways.

When an **async** function is called, the function's code is not executed immediately. Instead, the code in the function gets scheduled for execution at some future time. So what gets returned to the caller? A future that will be completed when the function's body is done, successfully or not. The function manufactures the future automatically and immediately returns that future to the caller.

Clearly, this relieves the programmer from writing a certain amount of boilerplate code, but the real value of **async** functions is that they can contain **await** expressions.

8.6.1 Await

An *await expression* allows one to write asynchronous code almost as if it were synchronous. Executing an **await** expression lets us suspend the surrounding function while we wait for an asynchronous computation to finish.

Recall our example from Section 8.2.1, where we wanted to test that the copy() method of File worked as advertised. Using **await**, we can write the assertion as:

```
assert((await myFile.copy(myPath)).path == myPath);
```

which is very close to what we would write if copy was synchronous:

```
assert(myFile.copy(myPath).path == myPath);
```

and more direct than the version using futures explicitly:

myFile.copy(myPath).then((f){**assert**(f.path == myPath);});

An **await** can only be used within an **async** function. The Dart compiler will not accept an **await** elsewhere.

When thinking about the execution of an **async** function, one needs to remember that its body has been scheduled for execution independently of its caller, in a later turn. So when the **async** function is running, its caller is long gone. In particular, when debugging, there is no meaningful call stack to refer to—and there is no caller to return to. So what does a **return** statement mean inside an **async** function? All a **return** can do is complete the future associated with an **async** function with a value. As usual, a **return** without a nested expression is treated as a shorthand for **return null;**. Likewise, if an **async** function throws an exception that it does not catch, the function's future is completed with the object thrown.

8.6.2   Asynchronous Generators

Asynchronous generators are another form of asynchronous function supported by Dart. A function whose body is marked with the **async*** modifier acts as a generator function (4.8) for a stream. The idea is best illustrated via an example. The following function produces a stream containing the natural numbers in sequence:

```
get naturals async* {
  int k = 0;
  while (true) {
    yield await k++;
  }
}
```

When naturals is called, it immediately returns a new stream. Once that stream is listened to, the function body is run in order to generate values to populate the stream. The function runs in an infinite loop. Each iteration executes a **yield** statement, which has an **await** inside it. The **await** increments k and suspends the function.

Later, the function is resumed with a new value of k, which **yield** appends to the stream. This process repeats on every iteration, adding the next natural number to the stream. Of course, this isn't a very good way to produce this sequence; the function is run at most once every cycle through the event loop.

Here is a more realistic example, which obtains data in chunks over HTTP and places it on a stream. The function getRepeatedly is called with a URI uri and a number *n* indicating how many times the URI should be accessed:

```
Stream getRepeatedly(uri, n) async* {
  for (var i = 0; i < n; i++) {
    var response = await http.get(uri);
    var nextJson = json.convert(response.body);
    yield nextJson;
```

```
    await new Future.delayed(new Duration(seconds: 2));
  }
}
```

A stream is returned to the caller immediately. Once the stream is listened to, the body of getRepeatedly will begin running. It will loop n times; each iteration will access the URI provided using **await** to obtain a response asynchronously and suspend. After the response is ready, the function will resume. The response is converted to JSON and posted to the stream that was returned to the caller. Then the function waits for two seconds and starts the next iteration.

8.6.3 Await-For loops

Given a stream, one can loop over its values:

```
await for (var i in naturals) { print('event loop $i'); }
```

Every time an element is added to the stream, the loop body is run. After each iteration, the function enclosing the loop suspends until the next element is available or the stream is done.

Just like **await** expressions, **await-for** loops may only appear inside asynchronous functions. The reasoning in both cases is the same: both constructs cause the surrounding function to suspend, and a function that suspends is no longer synchronous.

8.7 Related Work

Dart's model of isolates with their own memory is a variant of the actor model first proposed by Hewitt over 40 years ago[22], [23]. Since then, many variations on the actor model have been introduced in various languages, notably Erlang[24], E[25], Newspeak[26] and Scala[27]. As in E, Newspeak and the original actor model, Dart message passing is non-blocking.

The concept of a future in programming has many variants. These include the promises of E, the futures of Scala's actor library Akka and many others.

Dart's streams are heavily influenced by the work of Meijer on Rx[28]. Support for **async** methods and **await** expressions was inspired by the analogous constructs in C#. However, unlike C#, Dart **async** functions are always asynchronous, and Dart's **await** expressions always suspend the surrounding function.

8.8 Summary

Dart programs consist of one or more isolates, which are actor-like units of concurrency, each with its own memory and a single thread of control. Isolates are Dart's unit of concurrency and security. Isolates are non-blocking and communicate via asynchronous message passing. Message sends return futures representing their anticipated results. Futures support callbacks that specify what action to take when the future completes, either successfully or unsuccessfully. Streams provide a higher-level abstraction on which Dart applications are typically constructed. Finally, **async** methods make it possible to write asynchronous programs in a style not dissimilar to synchronous ones.

Chapter 9
Conclusion

What can we conclude from our grand tour of Dart? What have I learned in the process of working on Dart that might be worth conveying to you? What should have been done differently? In this brief chapter, we shall review the main lessons of Dart as it is, and Dart as it might be.

9.1 Optional Typing

Optional typing has been proposed in one form or another for decades. Dart is the first mainstream programming language to support optional typing from its inception. Shortly after Dart's introduction, a number of other languages appeared with similar features. It is not necessarily the case that these languages were directly inspired by Dart. However, it is clear that non-mandatory type systems are an idea whose time has come.

What is less clear is whether Dart represents the best approach in this space. Dart mandates a specific optional type system as part of the language specification. This has the advantage of establishing a lingua franca for types in Dart programs. On the other hand, the flexibility of optional and especially pluggable types[29] is maximized if types become part of the language tooling rather than part of the language itself. Extra-linguistic tools can evolve more quickly than the language can.

Checked mode has proven itself to be a double-edged sword. Its usefulness is very clear, but it comes at a price. Despite the argument that checked mode is only a development-time tool, it has tended to be treated as a de facto runtime type system, counter to the precept that the type system should not impact runtime semantics. In this book, we have seen this undesirable impact of checked mode when discussing proxies.

Another weakness of checked mode is that it is an all-or-nothing proposition. One might like to be able to activate checked mode at a fine grain, perhaps per-module or even per-function.

A sound (but optional) static type discipline would reduce the need for checked mode. A design with sound rules but without checked mode is closer to the original optional type system of Strongtalk, and might be an attractive alternative. Optional types can certainly be made sound. As usual, there are trade-offs involved. Dart has chosen to forego soundness to better cater to programmer intuition. However, sound analyses have important benefits. The closer we hew to the idea of truly optional (and hence pluggable) types, the more flexibility we have in choosing sound or unsound approaches as needed.

An interesting and unforeseen effect of optional typing has been increased user expectations. Once people realize that a program runs correctly despite type warnings, they demand more intelligence from the type system. Examples include flow-aware type rules and better inference.

Overall, users might be better served by moving types out of the domain of the language and into the domain of tools, allowing a rapidly evolvable mix of sound and unsound type systems with varying approaches to inference.

9.2 Object Orientation

Dart is a pure object-oriented language. All runtime values are objects, and for the most part this has worked very well.

However, some things are not runtime values in Dart, and consequently they are not objects. Libraries and prefixes are the obvious offenders here. Oddly, libraries and prefixes are often implemented as objects under the covers, and it is the language that undermines this regularity.

The consequences of treating libraries as full-fledged objects are profound. Precisely because the implications are so far-reaching, the idea has not been pursued in Dart. It challenges conventional ideas about module systems, and so runs counter to the goal of familiarity.

The price of using conventional modularity constructs is high, because conventional modularity constructs are woefully inadequate. We have encountered a litany of issues involving dependency-injection, flexible library configurations and dynamic loading. All of these could be resolved by a more radical design, as evidenced by Newspeak[30].

Classes are objects in Dart, but their functionality is limited. The decision to treat class methods and constructors as static features is a lost opportunity to leverage the uniformity of the pure object model. In a world where libraries and classes are objects, only one kind of method access (instance) is needed instead of three (top-level, class and instance). The simplification cascades through the system, from specification to implementation to tools.

Finally, there is a view that pure object orientation requires that the running program/system itself be an object. Such a point of view implies that reflection is integral to object orientation. Dart supports reflection, but not as well or as throughly as it could. The next section examines this topic.

9.3 Reflection

Dart's support for reflection is still evolving. At this point, it falls short of ideal. Programmers are routinely advised to avoid it, mainly due to pragmatic issues related to the size of deployed code. These issues were discussed in Chapter 7.

It is true that in some cases reflection is overused. Reflection has been especially over-utilized in support of dependency injection and for binding in user interface frameworks. It is regrettable that dependency injection is even needed in Dart. Powerful modularity techniques based on first-class libraries mentioned in the previous section would make dependency injection frameworks unnecessary.

On the other hand, the tendency to reach for reflection illustrates its value in terms of power and convenience. It is entirely possible to support reflection in an effective manner, as discussed in Section 7.4.

Going beyond introspection to dynamically evolving programs (7.5) is another area where reflection support in Dart is lacking. This has had a large impact on the overall Dart programming experience, as discussed in the following section.

9.4 Tooling

Programming involves much more than just an abstract notion of a programming language. The reality of programming involves language, implementation, libraries, tooling, culture and community.

Dart has had an ambition to deliver many of the advantages of Smalltalk to a wider audience. It has been heavily influenced by Smalltalk as mentioned throughout this book. However, the constraints on Dart in terms of familiarity and target implementation platform have tended to curtail that ambition.

The limitations have been most striking in the domain of tooling. There are a number of IDEs that offer support for Dart. In keeping with Dart's familiar feel, these IDEs are all very conventional in their design. None of them offer an experience remotely similar to a Smalltalk IDE. The Smalltalk ideals of live programming have enjoyed a renaissance in recent years, and future Dart development environments should correct this deficiency.

The live feel of Smalltalk is derived from a combination of metacircular tool design and the ability of programs to modify themselves as they execute. It is the ability of programs to change themselves over time, rather than dynamic typing, that really makes a programming language dynamic. Such dynamism can be achieved in a structured way via mirror builders (7.5).

Most Dart IDEs today are not written in Dart and do not address liveness. No amount of themes, plugins and options can replace the ability of the programmer to mold tools to their needs directly, and get instant feedback while they do so.

9.5 Summary

Dart is a programming language designed to be familiar and useful to a mainstream audience, while still attempting to adhere to the core principles of object-orientation: that the only thing that matters about an object is its behavior, that every runtime value is an object, and that the code of the program itself can be seen as an object and therefore reflected upon.

At the time of this writing, there are millions of lines of Dart code in use within Google, and millions more outside it. The language is clearly useful to many programmers; and it is clearly familiar.

In order to be familiar, Dart has not always adhered to the principles of object orientation as much as the author of this book would have liked. In order to be useful, it has largely focused on web programming, and that too has led to compromises.

Nevertheless, Dart has had an important impact on the world of programming. The world has grown accustomed to the idea of optional typing. The bar has been raised with respect to the performance one can expect from a dynamically typed pure object-oriented language. Programmers have a viable alternative to Javascript when programming in the web browser.

The success of Dart will be judged over time, as the language continues to evolve. One hopes it will improve in the process.

Bibliography

[1] A. Goldberg and D. Robson, *Smalltalk-80: The Language and Its Implementation.* Addison-Wesley, 1983.

[2] L. Bak, G. Bracha, S. Grarup, R. Griesemer, D. Griswold, and U. Hölzle, "Strongtalk website." http://www.cs.ucsb.edu/projects/strongtalk/.

[3] C. Unkel and M. S. Lam, "Automatic inference of stationary fields: A generalization of java's final fields," in *Proceedings of the 35th Annual ACM SIGPLAN-SIGACT Symposium on Principles of Programming Languages*, POPL '08, (New York, NY, USA), pp. 183–195, ACM, 2008.

[4] G. Bracha and W. Cook, "Mixin-based inheritance," in *Proc. of the Joint ACM Conf. on Object-Oriented Programming, Systems, Languages and Applications and the European Conference on Object-Oriented Programming*, Oct. 1990.

[5] G. Bracha and D. Griswold, "Extending Smalltalk with mixins," Sept. 1996. OOP-SLA Workshop on Extending the Smalltalk Language.

[6] L. Bak, G. Bracha, S. Grarup, R. Griesemer, D. Griswold, and U. Hölzle, "Mixins in Strongtalk," 2002. Invited paper, ECOOP Workshop on Inheritance.

[7] S. Krishnamurthi, M. Felleisen, and D. P. Friedman, "Synthesizing object-oriented and functional design to promote re-use," in *European Conference on Object-Oriented Programming*, pp. 91–113, Springer, 1998.

[8] M. Torgersen, "The expression problem revisited four new solutions using generics," in *European Conference on Object-Oriented Programming*, pp. 123–143, Springer-Verlag, 2004.

[9] M. Zenger and M. Odersky, "Independently extensible solutions to the expression problem," in *In Proc. FOOL 12*, 2005.

[10] A. Snyder, "Encapsulation and inheritance in object-oriented programming languages," in *Proc. of the ACM Conf. on Object-Oriented Programming, Systems, Languages and Applications*, pp. 38–45, 1986.

[11] A. Snyder, "Inheritance and the development of encapsulated software components," in *Research Directions in Object-Oriented Programming*, pp. 165–188, MIT Press, 1987.

[12] G. Bracha, *The Programming Language Jigsaw: Mixins, Modularity and Multiple Inheritance.* PhD thesis, University of Utah, 1992.

[13] N. Schärli, *Traits—Composing Classes from Behavioral Building Blocks.* PhD thesis, University of Berne, February 2005.

[14] R. B. Findler and M. Flatt, "Modular object-oriented programming with units and mixins," in *Proc. of the ACM SIGPLAN International Conference on Functional Programming,* pp. 94–104, 1998.

[15] M. Odersky, L. Spoon, and B. Venners, *Programming in Scala.* Mountain View, California: Artima Press, 2008.

[16] G. Bracha and D. Griswold, "Strongtalk: Typechecking Smalltalk in a production environment," in *Proc. of the ACM Conf. on Object-Oriented Programming, Systems, Languages and Applications,* Sept. 1993.

[17] O. L. Madsen, B. Møller-Pedersen, and K. Nygaard, *Object-Oriented Programming in the Beta Programming Language.* Addison-Wesley, 1993.

[18] B. Ford, "Parsing expression grammars: A recognition-based syntactic foundation," in *Proc. of the ACM Symp. on Principles of Programming Languages,* pp. 111–122, January 2004.

[19] D. Ungar and R. Smith, "SELF: The power of simplicity," in *Proc. of the ACM Conf. on Object-Oriented Programming, Systems, Languages and Applications,* Oct. 1987.

[20] G. Bracha and D. Ungar, "Mirrors: Design principles for meta-level facilities of object-oriented programming languages," in *Proc. of the ACM Conf. on Object-Oriented Programming, Systems, Languages and Applications,* Oct. 2004.

[21] G. Bracha, "Executable grammars in Newspeak," *Electron. Notes Theor. Comput. Sci.,* vol. 193, pp. 3–18, 2007.

[22] C. Hewitt, P. Bishop, and R. Steiger, "A universal modular actor formalism for artificial intelligence," in *Proceedings of the 3rd International Joint Conference on Artificial Intelligence,* IJCAI'73, (San Francisco, California), pp. 235–245, Morgan Kaufmann Publishers Inc., 1973.

[23] G. Agha, *Actors: A Model of Concurrent Computing in Distributed Systems.* Cambridge, Massachusetts: MIT Press, 1986.

[24] J. Armstrong, *Programming Erlang: Software for a Concurrent World.* Pragmatic Bookshelf, 2013.

[25] M. S. Miller, *Robust Composition: Towards a Unified Approach to Access Control and Concurrency Control.* PhD thesis, Johns Hopkins University, Baltimore, Maryland, May 2006.

[26] N. Botev, "Actor-based concurrency in Newspeak 4," 2012. San Jose State University Master's Projects Paper 231.

[27] P. Haller and F. Sommers, *Actors in Scala*. Artima, 2012.

[28] E. Meijer, "Your mouse is a database," *Commun. ACM*, vol. 55, no. 5, pp. 66–73, May 2012.

[29] G. Bracha, "Pluggable type systems," Oct. 2004. OOPSLA Workshop on Revival of Dynamic Languages. Available at http://pico.vub.ac.be/%7Ewdmeuter/RDL04/papers/Bracha.pdf.

[30] G. Bracha, P. von der Ahé, V. Bykov, Y. Kashai, W. Maddox, and E. Miranda., "Modules as objects in Newspeak," in *European Conference on Object-Oriented Programming*, June 2010.

Index

REGISTER YOUR PRODUCT at informit.com/register
Access Additional Benefits and SAVE 35% on Your Next Purchase

- Download available product updates.

- Access bonus material when applicable.

- Receive exclusive offers on new editions and related products.
  (Just check the box to hear from us when setting up your account.)

- Get a coupon for 35% for your next purchase, valid for 30 days. Your code will
  be available in your InformIT cart. (You will also find it in the Manage Codes
  section of your account page.)

Registration benefits vary by product. Benefits will be listed on your account page
under Registered Products.

InformIT.com—The Trusted Technology Learning Source
InformIT is the online home of information technology brands at Pearson, the world's foremost
education company. At InformIT.com you can

- Shop our books, eBooks, software, and video training.
- Take advantage of our special offers and promotions (informit.com/promotions).
- Sign up for special offers and content newsletters (informit.com/newsletters).
- Read free articles and blogs by information technology experts.
- Access thousands of free chapters and video lessons.

Connect with InformIT—Visit informit.com/community
Learn about InformIT community events and programs.

informIT.com
the trusted technology learning source

Addison-Wesley · Cisco Press · IBM Press · Microsoft Press · Pearson IT Certification · Prentice Hall · Que · Sams · VMware Press

ALWAYS LEARNING   PEARSON